The Developing Child

Recent decades have witnessed unprecedented advances in research on human development. Each book in The Developing Child series reflects the importance of this research as a resource for enhancing children's well-being. It is the purpose of the series to make this resource available to that increasingly large number of people who are responsible for raising a new generation. We hope that these books will provide rich and useful information for parents, educators, child-care professionals, students of developmental psychology, and all others concerned with childhood.

Jerome Bruner, New School for Social Research
Michael Cole, University of California, San Diego
Barbara Lloyd, University of Sussex
Series Editors

The Developing Child Series

Sisters and Brothers

Judy Dunn

Harvard University Press
Cambridge, Massachusetts
1985

Copyright © 1985 by Judy Dunn
All rights reserved
Printed in the United States of America
10 9 8 7 6 5 4 3 2 1

This book is printed on acid-free paper, and its binding materials
have been chosen for strength and durability.

Library of Congress Cataloging in Publication Data
Dunn, Judy
    Sisters and brothers.
    (The Developing child)
    Bibliography: p.
    Includes index.
    1. Brothers and sisters.   2. Sibling rivalry.
I. Title. II. Series.
BF723.S43D87 1985   155.4′43   84-19343
ISBN 0-674-80980-7 (alk. paper)
ISBN 0-674-80981-5 (pbk.: alk. paper)

For Jean

Contents

The
Developing
Child

Sisters and Brothers

1 / Introduction

Sally, aged six, talks about her sister Anny, aged three: "She's nice . . . sometimes nice. It's good to have a sister, because you can play with them . . . That's the only part of my life that I like, when I'm playing with her . . . I do have lots of friends but my best friend is Anny."

Rachel telephones her grandmother, announcing that she is writing her autobiography and needs help with punctuation. The autobiography begins with a list of her likes and dislikes. The list of dislikes is simple: "Violence, eggplant, and my brother."

Growing up with a sibling involves very different experiences for Sally and for Rachel, and the intensity of those experiences is clear from their strikingly different views. Young brothers and sisters love and hate, play and fight, tease and mock each other with devastating lack of inhibition. Some quarrel and bicker constantly; others are inseparable, affectionate companions; others veer between happy, cooperative play and fierce aggression. How do these experiences of a childhood spent with brothers and sisters influence the way in which children develop? Why should some siblings get along so well, and others fight and quarrel with such hostility? And why do brothers and sisters differ so much from one another?

Behind these questions lie two issues—themes that run throughout this book. One is the issue of whether brothers and sisters influence the way in which a child develops. The second is the issue of why some siblings relate to each other harmoniously and affectionately, and others constantly fight and argue.

For anyone interested in why people develop in the way that they do, these are serious issues. For parents, they certainly seem important. Should parents, for instance, feel responsible if their children quarrel constantly and seem to dislike each other? Books for parents often suggest that such behavior is primarily the result of the children's upbringing. Is this a reasonable view? How good is the evidence on which it is based? The fact that siblings within a family differ so much from one another also presents parents and psychologists with a real puzzle. Siblings are indeed almost as different in personality from one another as unrelated children brought up in different families. Why should this be? After all, brothers and sisters not only grow up in the same family environment, but they share 50 percent of their genes. Are the differences in their personalities the result of differences in the way that their parents have treated them, or could the siblings also influence each other directly? Having more than one child raises a host of questions for parents. How does a parent's relationship with one child affect the way the siblings get along together? Is the age gap between the children important? How does gender affect the way the children relate to each other? How well do brothers and sisters understand one another, and does a close relationship between them in early childhood continue as they grow up?

In this book we will be looking at these and other questions raised by the two themes, drawing upon some of the recent studies of young siblings to help us answer them. But we will also look well beyond the practicalities of coping with fights and arguments or the difficulties following the birth of a sibling to a third theme, which is the major "story" of the book. Watching and listening to young siblings and talking to them about their relationship give us a new and illuminating perspective on how children see and understand their world. In their games, their fights, their bullying, teasing, or comforting, children show us with splendid clarity that even in their early years their powers of understanding other people are often far greater than psychologists have supposed. If we study children in a setting that really matters to them—their family world of siblings and parents—we get a picture of their development that in some ways is startlingly different from the accepted view. The third theme of this book, then, is that by looking at siblings growing up together, watching the changes in the way that they fight and play, compete with and support each other, we gain vivid new insights into how children develop—emotionally, socially, intellectually.

Each of the three themes is important both to parents and to students of psychology, and the book is written for both audiences. The topics and studies with which we are concerned are illuminating for the practical insights they can give to parents, and for the insights they provide into the challenging questions of why children develop in the way that they do and what they understand and feel about their family world. Take, for instance, the issue of quarrels and hostility between siblings. This is discussed in Chapter 3, with respect to the third theme: What do the disputes between siblings show us about how children think and feel, and about how their understanding grows? In Chapter 7, however, quarrels are discussed within the framework of the second theme, emphasizing the practical problems of living with quarrelsome siblings. The practical problems may be of less interest to students than to parents (though to students who eventually will have care of children they are of real importance). But to stress disparities in the interests of different sets of readers of this Developing Child Series is misleading. There is a wide overlap between the audiences: most parents *are* psychologists—at least as far as their own children are concerned—and psychologists are very often parents. The three themes of the book are relevant to people who are fathers and mothers, and to those who are simply interested in why people develop as they do, whether they are "psychologists" or not. The final chapter returns to the questions raised by each of the three themes and to the implications of the research on siblings, both for parents and for psychologists.

Most children grow up with siblings—80 percent in the United States and Europe. The time they spend together in their early years is often far greater than the time they spend with their mothers or fathers. In many cultures children are brought up by their siblings: from the age of one or two they are nursed, fed, disciplined, and played with by a brother or sister only three or four years older than they. It is the beginning of a relationship that lasts a lifetime—longer indeed than that between husband and wife, or between parent and child. The first theme of this book concerns the question of how this experience of growing up with siblings affects a child's personality, the way he or she thinks about himself, his family and friends, his intelligence, and his ways of thinking and talking.

On commonsense grounds it seems very likely that it is important. Some psychologists argue, and parents would surely agree, that what children feel about and learn from other children can dramatically influence their development. Children are particularly likely to attend to and understand the feelings and viewpoints of their friends. When children talk to and argue with adults, they are at an obvious disadvantage: the way they see the world is different and their power, status, and understanding are limited, compared with those of adults. Between children there is greater equality. They are more likely to understand how other people who are children like themselves think or see things.

If we are to discover whether siblings *do* influence each other, and why it is that siblings differ so much from one another—a point that is obvious to parents, and that has now been carefully documented by scientists—then we clearly have to look *both* at the way parents treat their different children *and* at the way the children relate to one another. It could well be that children themselves influence each other in ways that increase the differences between them. One child may feel hostile toward and irritated with his sister, jealous of her relationship with their parents, infuriated by her personality and her habits. His sister, in contrast, may be happy and easygoing about competing for parental attention, admiring of her brother's skills, eager to please, yet rebuffed when she tries. Growing up within the same family has very different meanings for the two: for one child the family includes someone who arouses irritation and takes parental attention and love; for the other there is someone to admire, care about, and learn from. And, of course, differences in how the children behave toward one another may be closely linked to differences in how the parents treat the different chilen, which may be either a cause or a consequence of the siblings' behavior.

If siblings do influence one another directly, this may

not necessarily increase the differences between them. Siblings may admire, imitate, and identify with one another, uniting in the face of problems and difficulties, emulating the qualities they like about each other. The point is that if we are to understand how patterns of personality develop, we must not ignore the possible influence of the children with whom individuals grow up and with whom they spend their early years—their sisters and brothers.

There have been plenty of theories, guesses, and hypotheses about how siblings influence each other, but until recently there was little careful research on early childhood; psychologists generally assumed that it is children's relationships with their parents (and especially with their mothers) that are of overwhelming importance. Parents, however, are often sure that they can pick out the ways in which their children affect one another. They also often believe that they have brought up their various children differently and that this has influenced the way in which the children have developed. Some find that they have always had a special delight and closeness with the firstborn; others, that with their second or third child they felt a warmth and relaxation that they could not bring to their relationship with their first.

What does recent research tell us about the relationships between siblings and parents? Throughout this book I have tried wherever possible to let the children and their parents speak for themselves, using direct quotations and observations. These vignettes and quotations are *not* simply anecdotes; they are used to illustrate points that have been established by systematic studies. Children talking about their own lives and families often make these points with more vigor and energy than cautious academics. But although the children's

comments and actions are sometimes poignant, sometimes funny, they are included not simply to amuse or
move but to highlight serious general findings from research. There is one set of exceptions to this. In Chapter
8, I discuss the importance of siblings in adolescence
and adulthood—a subject on which there is little systematic information. I have therefore drawn here on
letters and reminiscences to illustrate at a case-history
level how significant the experience of being a sibling
can be. For early childhood, in contrast, there is now
detailed systematic research on which to draw.

In the next chapters, then, we will look at the arguments, games, and discussions of young siblings, at the
children's own views of their brothers and sisters, and
at their parents' picture of their developing relationship.
Revealed in the experience of these young siblings—the
experience of learning to live with a challenging, exciting
companion, a rival for the parents' attention and love—
is a developmental story of great poignancy, a story of
how understanding and emotion grow and change. We
begin at the beginning, when the only child becomes a
firstborn, with the birth of a sibling.

2 / Siblings in Early Childhood

Firstborn children react to the birth of a sibling in very distinctive ways. Most of them show signs of being upset: sleep disturbances, frequent crying, toilet training breakdown, an inability to concentrate on play, and, above all, naughty and demanding behavior. These problems reflect the great emotional impact that the sibling's arrival has upon young children. But the presence of the new baby is not only a source of disturbance—it is of very great interest to most firstborn children.

In the early days after a sibling is born, firstborns show their interest in the baby in many different ways. Comments about the baby, attempts to entertain, and gallant efforts to join in the care of the baby are frequently made, even by children under two years old. Studies in the United States, Canada, and Great Britain have shown that imitation of the baby's grimaces, yawns, and sounds, curiosity about why the baby behaves in certain ways, and make-believe games about being a baby or mother are all common and reflect the interest that most firstborns show in a new sister or brother.

The intensity of this interest is recalled by the Russian writer Sergei Aksakoff, in his delightful *Years of Childhood*, first published in 1858:

My little sister I loved at first more than my toys, more than my mother; and this love took the form of a constant desire to see her: I always fancied that she was cold or hungry and in want of food, and I wished constantly to give her my food and dress her in my clothes; of course I was not allowed to do this and that made me cry . . . I could not bear to see her tears nor hear her cry without beginning at once to cry myself . . . I lay whole days in my crib with my sister beside me, amusing her with different toys or by showing her pictures.

But the same child who shows a friendly interest in entertaining and comforting the baby may sometimes deliberately cause irritation or distress—for instance, by throwing the baby's pacifier across the room, or by banging the crib till the baby wakes and cries. In studies that my colleagues and I carried out in Cambridge, England, this ambivalence was often explicit in the children's comments about the baby.

Laura W. and Mother
Laura to Baby: All right, baby [caressing him]. [to Mother] Smack him.

Fay G. and Mother
Fay: Baby. Baby [caressing her]. Monster. Monster.
Mother: She's not a monster.
Fay: Monster.

And several children clearly expressed their antagonism to the baby:

Marvin W. [standing on edge of pram, rocking it] and Mother
Mother: Don't stand on there, there's a good boy, or you'll tip her out.
Marvin: I want her out.

This ambivalence, seen in most firstborn children in the early weeks of the sibling relationship, has been commented on by psychologists studying siblings at all stages of childhood and adolescence. And it is very often noted by parents. As one Cambridge mother remarked, "It all comes down to love and hate, doesn't it?"

Direct hostility to a newborn sibling was not frequently shown in the studies carried out in the United States, Canada, and Britain, although aggression between toddlers, preschool-aged children, and older siblings was very common. In contrast, deliberate naughtiness and aggression toward the *mother* often increased dramatically after the birth of a sibling. One Cambridge study showed a threefold increase in incidents of naughtiness in the two to three weeks following the arrival of a sibling. (See Chapter 7 for a detailed discussion of the problems associated with the birth of a sibling.)

It is clear, then, that firstborn children are very interested in their newborn sibling, and that the baby's arrival and presence is a matter of great emotional importance. The stage is set for the relationship between the children to develop, and it is set in a way that suggests that this is not an emotionally neutral affair—that potentially this new relationship may be of great importance to the first child and also to the younger sibling, who will be growing up with a child who is intensely emotionally involved and vigilantly interested. With respect to the book's first theme (the issue of sibling influence on development), this interest and the emotional quality of the first child's behavior suggest, already, that the relationship may well be one in which the children affect one another's development.

Vigilant interest is particularly clear in the way in which

2 - interest in new siblings

firstborn children monitor the behavior of their mothers with the new baby. This was shown in the Cambridge studies: whenever the mother picked up the baby to cuddle or caretake, firstborns were particularly likely to do the one thing that their mothers had expressly forbidden or that particularly irritated them. Tipping out the baby's bathwater, fiddling with the television, investigating a forbidden kitchen cupboard—all occurred just when the mother was most absorbed in the baby. Two examples from the Cambridge studies: One child, whose mother and baby sister were gazing at each other in a long, absorbed exchange, picked up his cup, which had a lid with holes in it, and, looking across to the baby and his ecstatic, cooing mother, started to sprinkle his milk all over the sofa. A second child, watching his mother act in a similar way, ran into the garden and laughingly let down the line with a full load of clean wash onto the muddy grass.

Most firstborns are interested, at least in the first few days, in helping to look after their newborn sibling. Children as young as eighteen months try to join in bathing, feeding, and dressing the baby. Changing the baby and discussion of dirt, cleanliness, and bowel movements are often of great interest, as this dialogue from the Cambridge studies illustrates. Three-year old Melanie C. is talking with her mother:

Melanie: He doing pooh.
Mother: Yes, I thought that might interest you. Yeah. Well, leave his feet alone. You'll make him uncomfortable.
Melanie: He got pooh.
Mother: I don't think he's finished yet. We'll have to stand and wait for him.

Melanie: OK. OK. [peers closely at baby and pulls diaper]

Mother: No, don't, Melanie; let him finish first. We'll just stand here while he finishes. No, don't pull it.

Melanie to Baby: [in disgusted tone] Oh dear, Keith. Have you done pooh?

Mother: Well he has to do one sometime, doesn't he? Don't pull his legs off.

Melanie: Keith done a pooh . . . He finished, Mum?

Mother: I don't know.

Melanie: Do other one?

Mother: He's done two, hasn't he?

Melanie: Keith done next pooh. Mmm. Mmm. [starts to investigate diaper]

Mother: I'll clean that first, Melanie, thank you. I don't know if he's finished or not. [to Baby] Why don't you wait, eh?

Melanie to Baby: Why don't you wait?

Mother: I suppose he's being cooperative really. [to Baby] Have you finished? You're going to be sick now, aren't you? [to Melanie] I wouldn't put your hand in it if I were you . . . I shouldn't poke it. Give him a minute longer.

In other cultures, children play a large part in caring for their young siblings after infancy. A study of childcare in 186 societies for which detailed anthropological information is available has shown that 40 percent of infants were looked after by people other than their mothers, and that siblings were the main companions and caregivers. The ways in which siblings act as caregivers—the kind of responsibility and chores they are assigned, the age at which they are expected to "take over" the baby—vary greatly between cultures. Differences in the nature of the household and the community and in the cultural conception of children's maturity all influence what is expected of children as caregivers.

A detailed study of sibling care in Kenya, carried out by Bea Whiting and Carolyn Pope-Edwards, showed that child caregivers scolded, helped, fed, and gave attention to their baby and toddler siblings very much as adults do, but that they also played with them more and were more often aggressive. How does the experience of being brought up by a sibling affect a child's development? Can we use this information from other cultures to determine whether siblings influence one another? Several writers have speculated about these questions. Margaret Mead argued that the development of personality differences was restricted in cultures in which the children were primarily looked after by siblings. She assumed that siblings were less sensitively attuned to the individual characteristics of their charges than adults would have been. It has also been suggested that if children are looked after by their siblings they become less attached to their mothers. But much more systematic information is needed in order to test these arguments. The very wide variation in the nature of sibling caregiving must certainly be taken into account before we come to any generalizations about its consequences. The one finding that seems reasonably well established is that children who spend most of their early years in the care of young siblings tend to learn to talk later than those who are brought up by adults.

In the United States and Europe, young children are rarely given such extensive responsibility for their baby siblings. But in many families they do make some attempts to look after them and are much concerned at their distress. In their concern and their efforts to comfort, we see the first signs of the understanding that children show in their behavior toward their siblings (the third theme of this book). To recognize that another person is upset and to attempt to alleviate the other's distress is strikingly sophisticated behavior for such young children.

One study, set in a laboratory playroom, looked specifically at how four-year-olds acted when their young siblings were distressed at separation from the mother. Over half of the four-year-olds tried to comfort and reassure the toddlers and their actions were both prompt and effective.

In an everyday sense, then, there is often a friendly bond between very young children and their siblings— cooperative behavior, concern at distress. Can this bond be seen as an "attachment" in the sense in which John Bowlby and Mary Ainsworth have used the term for the relationship between parent and child? Can one child provide a secure base for the other, be missed when absent, and be used as a source of comfort and security? The answer is yes, but not in all families. Two important studies of attachment, one in Scotland and one in Uganda, showed that it was common for babies to become attached to their older siblings. We don't know if this attachment followed an earlier attachment to the mother. In the Cambridge studies, 50 percent of the babies at fourteen months were reported to miss an absent older sibling, and two thirds of these were said to miss their older brother or sister very much. And even at eight months several of the babies were devoted to their older siblings:

Mother of Siobhan F.: She thinks he's marvelous. Hero-worships him. If he plays with her foot, she kills herself laughing. She doesn't cry till he goes out of the room.

Mother of Jackie E.: She misses him a great deal if he isn't there. Shouts till she hears him in the morning. Fusses till she can see him. I'm not enough.

Several of the fourteen-month-olds went to their older siblings for comfort:

Mother of Ian and Graham W.: Graham goes to him for love and comfort. Saying "ah" and screwing up his face as if to say "Isn't he sweet!" Ian often comforts him, and he's very concerned when he's upset.

What is particularly notable is that some of the *secondborn* children, as young as fourteen, fifteen, or sixteen months, attempted to comfort their older siblings. This is strikingly sophisticated behavior for such young children.

Very young brothers and sisters provide security for babies who are in an unfamiliar place. Observations of children who were placed in a residential nursery showed that the children were much less distressed when they were admitted with an older sibling. Experiments tell the same story. In the study of babies who were separated from their mothers in a laboratory playroom, the babies whose siblings attempted to comfort them were calmed and reassured by their siblings, and started to play happily even though their mothers had not returned. When a stranger came into the room, most of the babies moved closer to their sibling, and from this safe base smiled happily at the stranger. In another study, babies, aged sixteen to twenty-two months, explored further away from their mothers when their older brothers or sisters were present.

Even children as young as two or three years can effectively comfort and take care of their baby siblings if they wish. But do they look after the baby and talk to him as a mother would—or do they treat the baby as if he were a child of their own age? Do they make adjustments in their speech and behavior that are appropriate for a small baby? Studies of the speech of very young children talking to their younger siblings show that children make many of the same "baby talk" adjustments that mothers do. In the Cambridge studies, children talked in much shorter sentences to their baby siblings than they did to their mothers; they repeated their comments and used lots of attention-getting features, just as a mother would. In the example below, Duncan, aged thirty-one months, is attempting to prevent his brother Robin, aged fourteen months, from eating a sweet that Robin has picked up off the floor. He tells him that the dog, Scottie, will eat it, then attempts to distract him by urging him to go into the kitchen. He finally pushes him through the door gently with his foot. The important point is that in his attempts to direct Robin, he uses all the devices that mothers do— he repeats his comments, shortens them progressively, and uses his brother's name to catch his attention:

> *Duncan K.:* No, don't you eat it. Scottie will eat it. Scottie will eat it. No, not you. Scottie will eat it. Not you. Scottie. Not you. Shall we go in door? Right. Come on. Come on. In door, Robin. In door.

Some of the children in the Cambridge study also used questions and endearments and diminutives in talking to their baby siblings, just as their mothers would have:

> *Ian W.:* [trying to get brother, Graham, to come and play in the next room with him] Come on, Gramie. Come on, tinkerwinker!

Eve D.: [showing sister, Kate, toys in a box] There, Kay-Kay, look! Kay-Kay, Kay-Kay, look! Kay-Kay! Kay-Kay! Look! Look, baby-baby.

Sara Harkness, studying children caregivers in Kenya with their two- and three-year-old charges, found that repetitions, explanations, and "language practice" speech were equally common in the speech of children caregivers and of mothers.

Preschool-aged children do make some appropriate and effective adjustments in the way they talk to their baby siblings. They do not, of course, provide the same kind of model for children learning to talk that mothers do; in fact, children who spend a great deal of time with other children tend to acquire language more slowly than those who spend most of their time with adults. But when young children wish to communicate with other very young children, they can do so with great effectiveness.

Studies of children's behavior toward their very young siblings have shown, clearly, that most young children are very interested in the babies. In many cultures they are responsible caregivers, and by the end of the first year many babies are attached to their older siblings and are delighted to see them and play with them. Play between the baby and the older sibling increases in frequency during the first year, and by seven or eight months the *salience* of the first child for the baby is obvious both in the attention the baby gives to the sibling and in the excitement with which he plays with, "talks to," and imitates the older child. Imitating the older sibling becomes more and more common: during the first eight months or so the older child more often imitates the baby, but by the time the baby is one year old it is the other way around. As the children grow up, this imitation becomes even more frequent. In a Canadian study by Rona Abramovitch and her colleagues, 20 percent of the interactions between twenty-month-old secondborn children and their older siblings involved imitation.

This copying of an older brother or sister is interesting for a number of different reasons. Consider the next example:

> Tom, fourteen months old, watches his older brother Ned put a toy pilot in a toy airplane, and "fly" it. Ned removes the pilot and shortly afterward leaves the room. Tom moves quickly to the plane, takes the pilot, puts him in the plane, and "flies" it.

In this example, the younger sibling, in imitating his older brother, is playing at a much more mature level than when he plays on his own. Tom, at fourteen months, is very young to be playing with pretend people as if they were carrying out actions like flying planes. We do not yet know whether imitations such as these are in fact *generally* important in the development of children's intellectual skills, but it certainly seems likely that they *can* be, as in the case of Tom. Imitation of an older sibling shows very clearly that siblings can indeed have a direct influence on how children play and on their skills with the world of objects.

Children copy their siblings in many other ways. Often a child will imitate an action by a brother or sister which has drawn the attention of an adult—even if this attention involved scolding or punishment. By eighteen months, secondborn children, after watching a dispute between their mother and older sibling over a forbidden action by the older child, will often immediately copy the prohibited act, laughing and looking at their mother while doing so. This delight in the transgression of a social rule—the new awareness of what is allowed and what is not—is very clearly shown in these imitations of the sibling's naughty actions. And as parents know so well, firstborn children often imitate their siblings' babyish actions or noises which draw the delighted attention of their parents.

There is yet another distinctive feature of the imitation between brothers and sisters that deserves mention. In games between very young siblings, often one child will imitate the other's actions—a bounce, a jump, a chant, a funny gesture—and then both children will continue to act together with shrieks of laughter. Here is an example from a Cambridge study.

> Judy B. puts her hand on the high chair where Carole [eight months] is sitting. Judy wiggles her fingers on the tray on the high chair. Carole watches. Judy wiggles her fingers; both continue to wiggle their fingers together, with mutual gaze and laughter. Three minutes later Carole, still in the high chair, wiggles her fingers on the tray, looks at Judy, and vocalizes.

Games of this kind, in which both children act together, are often played with great amusement and laughter. It is not clear why acting together should be such a source of excitement and pleasure. But it is interesting to note that these games happen more in families in which the first child has been warm and affectionate toward the baby sibling from the early weeks, and that in these families the firstborns are particularly likely to imitate the baby when she is small. Since we know that babies are particularly interested in people who are very responsive to their actions (whose behavior is closely linked to their own in time) and that they imitate people who are particularly nurturant or powerful, it is not surprising that it is in such families that the secondborn children come to imitate their older siblings frequently, and join in their actions with enthusiasm. Once the baby begins to imitate the older child, presumably the rewards to the older child as a model for this attentive and easily pleased audience increase.

But there is another possible explanation for the excitement expressed by the children in these imitative games: the pleasure the children show might reflect in part some recognition that the older child is "like me." Psychologists have shown that with older children, adolescents, and adults, individuals are more attracted to people whom they feel are "like me."

To react to someone as "like me" involves, of course, some elaborate categorization of both the self and the other person. It may seem inappropriate to suggest that children under three can think about themselves and others in this way. But one piece of evidence from the Cambridge studies which supports the idea is that these imitative games were much more common among same-sex sibling pairs. The intriguing possibility is that the *babies* were also more interested in the older siblings because they recognized, even at the beginning of the second year, that the older sibling was "like me" in terms of sex. If this is so, then it suggests again that children show remarkably mature behavior in the context of sibling relationships.

Imitation between very young siblings, then, shows us not only the closeness with which the children watch each other and the potential of the older as a model for the younger, but also the special excitement engendered in games when both simultaneously act together. Friendly, playful exchanges are in fact frequent between young siblings—notwithstanding the emphasis on rivalry that is found in much writing about siblings—and the friendly behavior of younger to older siblings increases as the children grow up, at least during the first three years of life. The children not only cooperate in games and show physical affection for each other; they often show concern at the other's distress and make practical attempts to help and comfort.

Aggression is, of course, frequent too. In one Canadian study, 29 percent of the behavior observed between siblings was hostile. Usually it was the older child being aggressive to the younger sibling, but as the secondborn children grew up they became increasingly aggressive as well.

The pattern of friendly and aggressive behavior between siblings highlights two important features of the children's behavior. First, whereas some children are primarily aggressive toward their siblings and others are usually friendly and rarely aggressive, many children show both frequent friendly and frequent hostile behavior toward their brothers and sisters. It would clearly be a mistake to describe the relationship between these children along a single dimension of warmth-hostility, since many show ambivalence rather than simply friendliness or aggression. Second, in many encounters between brothers and sisters, one child may be friendly and the other indifferent or hostile. This "mismatch" of emotions is important. Earlier I emphasized that there are striking differences between siblings in personality and behavior (the second theme of this book) and suggested that one possible way in which these differences between children reared within the same family might arise is through differences in the way in which children behave toward one another. Observations of very young siblings provide the first evidence that such differences in behavior may indeed be quite common. In one Cambridge study, 21 percent of interactions between first-borns and their fourteen-month-old brothers and sisters were "mismatches"—interactions in which one child was friendly, the other hostile.

To the book's first question—Do siblings influence each other?—we have the beginnings of some answers, even in the very first months of the sibling relationship. Just as the stage is set in the first weeks by the first child's *emotional* reaction to the new baby, so too the story of their relationship develops in strongly emotional terms. The salience of each child's behavior for the other, the imitation and modeling, the emotional power of their interactions—all suggest that even in the first two years the sibling is an important influence for both firstborn and laterborn children. Observations of mismatch interactions provide the first evidence that growing up with a sibling may be a very different experience for each child within a family, and may well contribute to the striking differences between siblings.

For our third theme—the understanding that children demonstrate in the context of the sibling relationship—observations of early sibling relationships are particularly revealing. The friendly and aggressive behavior of the children toward one another gives us a vivid picture of the beginnings of social understanding—the beginnings of children's grasp of the particular feelings, intentions, and needs of persons other than themselves, and of the social rules of the family in which they are growing up. When children show concern at their siblings' distress, fetch their comfort objects, offer those objects, and stroke their siblings affectionately, they have clearly grasped something of the nature of others' feelings and have some practical understanding of how to comfort them. Children begin to show these kinds of empathetic behavior toward their siblings during the second year—much earlier than empathy has been demonstrated using more formal tests of children's understanding of the feelings of other people. And in the context of conflict between siblings, children often show quite clearly that they know how to annoy and provoke another person. Take, for instance, these examples of teasing behavior from our studies:

> Anne, three years old, is playing with her teddy bear, her favorite comfort object. She is making a tent for him in the kitchen with a chair and a cloth. Eric, her younger brother, watches. Five minutes later both children are in the front room, and they have a fight over the possession of a toy car. Anne wins the fight. Eric is angry. He runs back to the kitchen, pulls Anne's tent to pieces, and hurls the teddy bear across the room. Anne bursts into tears.

> The mother of Elly and Andrew is telling a visitor in the kitchen that Elly [five years old] is frightened of spiders. "And there's a particular toy spider that she just hates," the mother comments. Andrew runs out of the kitchen, goes to the playroom, searches through the toy box, and finds the toy spider. He runs back to the kitchen and pushes the toy spider in Elly's face. Elly cries, Andrew laughs.

Andrew and Eric in these examples behave in a way that suggests they understand how to irritate their older siblings. Yet they are both only sixteen months old, an age at which psychologists have assumed that children have very little conception of the wishes and feelings of other people.

Why should such young children display relatively sophisticated understanding of their siblings? Why should they be able to comfort and to annoy a brother or sister well before they are two, whereas more formal tests of the ability to understand the perceptions and feelings of others suggest that such understanding begins only when children are four or five? There are a number of possible explanations for the discrepancy between observations of brothers and sisters together and more formal tests.

First, it is probably important that children are so familiar with their siblings—children they see every day in routinely familiar situations, whose reactions and actions they watch daily. Second, it is also probably important that what annoys, excites, and pleases a sibling frequently has the same effect on the child himself; sources of pleasure, joy, and fear are very similar for them. Third, it is important to consider the emotional context in which brothers and sisters play, talk, and fight with one another. It is a setting of real emotional urgency, and the depth of conflict, jealousy, or affection between the children should not be ignored in trying to explain why children grasp so early the feelings and intentions of their siblings. It *matters* very much to young children that they should understand what their siblings are feeling or intending to do.

This means that the sibling relationship is not only a context in which the extent of the children's social understanding is revealed with particular clarity, but that it is a context in which such understanding is likely to be fostered. The drama of conflict and the excitement of cooperation with a sibling provide a very important setting in which the child's understanding of other people begins to grow. To illustrate this point, let us look more closely at the changes in children's quarrels with their sisters and brothers over the first two or three years, and at the ways in which they cooperate in pretend play.

3 / Conflict, Play, and the Growth of Understanding

Compare the actions of Ben, a secondborn child, and his brother Dan in the following examples:

> Dan, aged two and a half, seizes a toy car from Ben, aged fourteen months, shouting, "I'm having this!" Ben begins to cry, looks at his mother, holds up his arms to be picked up.

> Ben, now aged eighteen months, is playing with a balloon. Dan approaches, and takes the balloon away, saying, "I want all the yellow ones." Ben screams, points at Dan while looking at his mother, shakes his head repeatedly, then goes to her and pulls her skirt. Then he runs at Dan and pushes at him violently.

> Ben, at twenty-one months, is playing with a cardboard box he is using as a garage. Dan approaches and says, "The fire engine is mine," and takes it away. Ben shouts, "No! No!" Then he runs over to the corner of the room where Dan has been constructing a castle of blocks for his favorite toy soldiers. He knocks down the castle, picks up the toy men, and throws them out of the room.

The changes in the way Ben behaved at fourteen, eighteen, and twenty-one months reflect a number of very important changes in his understanding of his brother, in his own aggressive behavior, and his grasp of how to elicit help from his mother. By twenty-one months he appears to know that taking Dan's toy soldiers will make Dan very upset, and he uses this understanding in situations in which Dan is frustrating him. The way in which he draws his mother's attention to Dan's behavior in the second example reflects both the expectation that his mother will come to his aid and his increased skill at enlisting her aid. By twenty-four months, children are often quite explicit about the transgression of social rules that their older sibling's behavior reflects.

> Tim, aged three and a half years, is eating a biscuit [cookie]. His mother accuses him of taking *her* biscuit: "Tim! That's my biscuit." "No, it isn't!" Tim replies. "Yes, it is, Tim. You're eating my biscuit," says his mother. Jill, aged twenty-four months, watches this exchange. Then she picks up a block and throws it at Tim. It hits him on the forehead and he begins to cry. His mother turns in surprise to Jill, who is normally a devoted and adoring younger sister, and says, "Why did you do that?" Jill replies, "Bad boy."

This incident, from the Cambridge studies, was a particularly striking one, as the two children in the family were a close and affectionate pair. Jill almost never showed aggressive or hostile behavior toward her brother, who was very sweet to her. In this instance she was quite explicit about the fact that he had transgressed a social rule by eating his mother's cookie.

Paralleling the changes in children's understanding of their siblings' wishes and intentions and of the social rules of the family—what is allowed and what is not—are changes in the anger and upset which children display during fights and quarrels with their siblings. Whereas at fourteen months most children burst into tears when their older siblings push them down or take their toys, by eighteen months they are much more likely to hit back, and indeed are often the first to hit, push, or pull hair. They frequently are the ones responsible for escalating the conflict to real physical violence. It is often hard on the older sibling, who is increasingly aware that he or she *must not* hit or bite the "baby," to realize that this "baby" is becoming a fierce and effective fighter and is less likely to be scolded in their quarrels. During their second year, children not only show more physical aggression in quarrels with their siblings, but they also act more violently when frustrated, whether by toys or by other people. They hurl objects across the room, destroy toys, bite themselves, and tend increasingly to express their anger in full-blown tantrums.

The parallel between these changes in displayed emotion and the child's understanding of how to annoy, upset, and frustrate the older brother or sister may well be important. When an older sibling snatches a toy, for example, there is a marked difference between the reaction of a one-year-old, a general distress, and the frustration shown by an eighteen- or twenty-four-month-old—an anger that *this person* can act this way toward me. A new vindictiveness is shown: I'm going to get back at *this person* in a way that will hurt *him*. It is also likely that children begin to use their emotional displays manipulatively in arguments, both with siblings and with parents, to get their own way. Certainly that is how it frequently seems to parents.

As children grow up, the nature of their fights changes. Though all too often a quarrel may end in the pushing, shoving, and hair pulling of the earlier years, many arguments take on a different form. Listen to the disputes between a three-year-old and an older sibling. Not only do teasing and harassment become increasingly sophisticated, but the younger child's powers of resolving the argument amicably also begin to develop. You may well hear not only the older but the younger brother making concessions, negotiating for an agreement, bargaining and offering alternative solutions to the dispute. There is a change, too, from simple prohibition—"Stop it!" "Don't!" "Shut up!"—to commands in which the child justifies his action in terms of rules that both share and understand. "That one's mine. Yours is the yellow one." "It's my turn, you've had a go. Mummy said we must share."

These skills of argument are shown occasionally even by two-year-olds, though conciliatory moves are very rare with such young children. The important point is that in verbal dispute the children are beginning to develop powers of argument that take account of the other child's point of view. Mothers, of course, frequently play a central role in mediating the disputes, encouraging each child to understand what the other child wants, to be patient, to anticipate the other's behavior.

Conflict between brothers and sisters not only shows clearly how well young children understand each other, but it may also be of special significance in fostering the growth of this understandinng. It may provide a crucial context in which children begin to grasp the social rules of their family world. To argue that conflict and quarrels can be important in this way is not to suggest that this is the *only* way in which children begin to understand each other and their family world. Brothers and sisters can be very close companions in play, riotous physical games, and intense, elaborate fantasies, and a close look at this shared make-believe play shows what a striking opportunity it provides for the children to explore the roles and rules of their world.

PRETEND PLAY

In some families playing pretend games can fill, as one mother put it, "95 percent of the children's waking day"; in other families pretend play between siblings is much less common. Two recent studies report that in families with two-year-olds and older siblings, roughly 60 percent of the two-year-olds' pretend-play episodes involved the mother, or the sibling, or both. If we compare the make-believe games that such young children play with their siblings and their mother, some striking differences become apparent.

First, while all different kinds of pretend play, from the simplest to the most elaborate, were played by children with their siblings, the way in which children cooperated with their siblings differed greatly from the way in which they played with their mothers. Mothers tended to act as spectators in the make-believe, offering suggestions or comments but not entering the games as full participants. Mothers' suggestions were usually concerned with making the make-believe as "real" as possible—as close as possible to the real-life situation which was the focus of the child's play. "Is that how it is in real life?" seems to be the theme of most mothers' contributions.

In make-believe with the sibling, in contrast, both children usually cooperated as partners in the fantasy. This collaboration between child and sibling was very striking in one respect: about a quarter of the two-year-olds in the studies joined their brothers and sisters in games that involved their taking on a *pretend identity* or playing at being in a *pretend place*. Children only two years old have been thought to be quite unable to make this kind of intellectual move. Yet consider these two examples from the Cambridge studies. In the first John, two years old, playing with his older sister Anne, takes on the role of "daddy" as instructed by Anne, answers appropriately when Anne calls him by his real father's name, and announces to the observer that he is a daddy.

Anne: I know, you can be the daddy and I can be the mummy. Yes?
John: Yes.
Anne: Right, we've got a baby, haven't we?
John: Yeah.
Anne: [addresses him by real father's name] Henry.
John: Yeah?
Anne: Have you got any babies?
John: [inaudible reply]
John: [to observer] I a daddy.

In the next example, two-year-old Laura is playing "mother" to her older sister, Carole.

Carole: [lying on her back] Change my bottom, Laura. Change my bottom.
Laura: Yes [pulls her pants off]. That's stinky! . . . Wee-wee! Wee-Wee!
Carole: Yes. Put some cream on here.
Laura: Come on Baby. I put the cream on. Get in [pretend bed] . . . [gives "food"].
Mother: What you doing? What you giving her?
Carole: She's giving me an egg. [to Laura] Give me more egg.
Laura: She ate my egg! I got no more left.
Carole: [high voice] Mum, I want that bib. Bib. Bib.
Laura: Which one?
Laura: [pretends to read book to baby] I read. I read.

Laura is cooperative (as John was in the first example), following her sister's directions to change her, but she also makes new additions to the game. She feeds her sister as the "baby," and reads to her from an imaginary book. Of course, it is possible that these are sequences which the two-year-olds have played repeatedly with their siblings, and that the older sibling had originally suggested the innovative actions to the two-year-olds in previous games. (In fact, a year later, when Laura was three, she and Carole were still enjoying the game in which Carole was the baby and Laura the mother.) But the examples show without question the ability of the two-year-olds to cooperate within the fantasy framework and to make explicit reference to the role identity which they had taken on.

Older brothers and sisters are almost always responsible for setting up and organizing these games when the younger siblings are as young as two, though by three the younger siblings are well able to suggest and organize games. The older siblings frequently keep up a running commentary on what is to happen in the pretend play, taking a strong-handed managerial role in the game with instructions (in an ordinary voice) interspersed with comments made in the play voice of the role they are enacting. The next three examples, drawn from the Cambridge studies, illustrate this management by the older siblings:

Kathy: [as teacher] Here comes your teacher. [in an exaggerated play voice] I'm going to read a story now, teacher. [switches to ordinary voice] No, you can't sit there, you'll have to sit just facing me. All right, sit here and I'll read you a story.

John: [in ordinary voice] Off now. No, you must still drive. [switches to exaggerated play voice] Thank you very much, see you later . . . [in ordinary voice] Get in now, you get in—get in the driving seat. Right.

No, Lenny [shouts] that's not the driving seat! That's
it! . . . Not yet. Come on. Get off. Go on! [shouting].

Kate: [in ordinary voice] Laura, talk just like Peter [a
friend]—say [adopts high-pitched "baby" voice], Can
I have some more sweeties? . . . [in authoritarian
"mother's" voice] Look, boys and girls, good girl, good
girl, go to sleep . . . now pick up your sandals. Good
girls, babies.

Although the two-year-olds seldom negotiate the roles
they are given in these games, they sometimes manage
to do so. Four-year-old Nell in the next example has
three imaginary friends, a remarkable trio called Lily,
Allelujah, and Peepee. Her two-year-old sister, Rose,
announces that she is Allelujah and when Nell disputes
this, Rose continues to tease her by repeating the an-
nouncement that *she* is Allelujah.

Rose: Allelujah! Allelujah! Me Allelujah!
Nell: Who's Allelujah?
Mother: Rose thinks she's Allelujah.
Nell: Who's Lily? Who's Lily?
Mother: I don't know. You tell me.
Nell: Who's Lily, Mummy?
Rose: I'm Allelujah.
Nell: [to Rose] Who's Lily? I'm Allelujah.
Rose: No, *I'm* Allelujah.

Later in the observation, Rose teased her sister by repeatedly announcing that she was Allelujah.

How important is the experience of playing with an
older sibling in the development of these abilities? It
was clear from the Cambridge studies that several of
the firstborns tried to engage their baby siblings in role-

play well before they were two, and their attempts were sometimes successful. Mary, in the next example, is only eighteen months. Her older sister has set up a birthday party game, making a birthday cake in the sandpit in the garden. Both children sing "Happy Birthday."

Kelly: Dear Mary! You're three now.

Mary: [nods] Mmm.

Kelly: You can go to school now.

Mary: [nods] Mmm.

Kelly: Do you want to go to school now?

Mary: Mmm.

Kelly: All right then. [play voice] Hello Mary. I'm Mrs. Hunt. Do you want to help me do some of this birthday cake, do you? [ordinary voice] We'd better help do our birthday cake, hadn't we?

Mary: [sings appropriately] "Happy Birthday . . ." [both children walk hand in hand around the garden singing]

Kelly: We're at church now. We have to walk along. I'm like Mummy and you're like Baby. I'm Mummy. [play voice] What, little one? We'd better go back to our birthday then.

Mary: [sings again] "Happy Birthday . . ." [Mary holds her hands up to her sister to be carried]

Kelly: [play voice] That's all right little girl. Are you going to sleep?

In some families the young brothers and sisters play together constantly in this way, and in other families they rarely if ever do so. It is in those families in which the children have a very warm and close relationship that they tend to cooperate and share pretend games in this way. Of course, it is possible that the experience of sharing this play *in itself* contributes to the closeness that develops between the children. Whatever the direction of influence, it is clear that in the context of a warm relationship with an older brother or sister, children can discover and explore in play the power and delight of transforming their identity and sharing a world of pretend. The two-year-olds in the Cambridge studies took on the identities not only of train engineers, mothers, fathers, and babies, but of airline pilots, motorists, policemen, shoppers, and a range of (often bizarre) imaginary friends.

How important these experiences are in the long-term development of children we can only speculate. But other studies of individual differences in pretend and symbolic play suggest that a rich fantasy life in childhood is linked with the development of a creative imagination and expressive powers in adulthood. The Brontë sisters and their brother provide one notable example, and another writer, Simone de Beauvoir, has written explicitly about the significance of her early pretend games with her sister, and the essential part her sister played in these: "The games I was fondest of were those in which I assumed another character, and in these I had to have an accomplice . . . A partner was absolutely essential to me if I was to bring my imaginary stories to life . . . In fact I was always the one who expressed myself through them; I imposed them on my sister, assigning her the minor roles which she accepted with complete docility."

Sergei Aksakoff also recalls in *Years of Childhood* the pleasure of fantasy games that he played with his sister, and the importance of this flattering (if incomprehending) companion in his games:

> Our poor town garden could not satisfy me . . . I often described to my sister different wonders which such an old traveller as I had witnessed; and she listened with

curiosity, fixing her pretty eyes full of rapt attention on me, while their expression clearly said, "Brother, I don't understand a word." Nor was that surprising as the narrator was just five years old and the sister three . . . Every day I gave my sister a reading lesson; this was a complete failure as she had not mastered even the alphabet; every day I made her listen while I read "Reading for Children," taking all the stories and articles in order even though there were many which I could not understand myself. My poor little listener often yawned and sometimes fell asleep while I read, and then I played games with her, building towns and churches of our bricks, or houses, of which the inhabitants were her dolls . . . this gave rise to many conversations and entertainments in complete imitation of grown-up people . . . I was much flattered by the impression which these narratives produced on my sister.

Watching the development of conflict and pretend play between siblings shows us with particular clarity the changes in children's understanding of their siblings.

In their relationship with their siblings, children display powers of understanding far greater than those that have been attributed to them on the basis of experimental studies. To comprehend why they should understand each other so well, we must certainly acknowledge the emotional power of the sibling relationship. If you compete for parental love with someone, it really matters that you should be able to anticipate his or her actions and intentions and to read his or her moods and feelings. In the vindictiveness and the precision with which children tease their siblings, we see not only that conflict *reveals* the human understanding of which even very young children are capable; we see, too, that this conflict behavior is driven by an emotional power that is very likely to *foster* such understanding.

The observations of brothers and sisters playing together highlight quite a different story. Clearly there is great power and attraction in play with another child who is friendly, who is close in interests, and who can share a pretend world. The maturity of such play and the excitement that it engenders again suggest that in the context of the relationship between brothers and sisters, children's understanding of their social world is not only revealed but fostered in the first years of childhood.

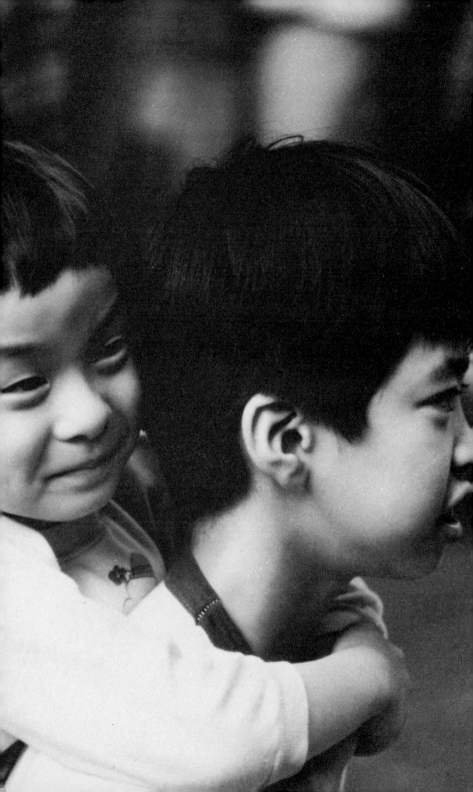

4 / The Early School Years

How do most school-aged children view their siblings? Six-year-old Sally, quoted at the beginning of this book, saw her sister Annie as her best friend. Is this common?

In the preschool years the intensity of the relationship between young brothers and sisters is clear—in their fighting, playing, teasing, sharing, and supporting. What happens as the children grow up and enter school, as they begin to form important friendships with other children? Does a close sibling relationship in the first years continue to be affectionate and important to the children as they grow up? Children's understanding of themselves and of the people in their world changes enormously between the preschool years and the early school years. How do these developments affect the relationship between brothers and sisters?

If you talk to children about their brothers and sisters, it is immediately apparent that the dramatic individual differences which are so obvious in the preschool years are still very marked. More than two decades ago Helen Koch interviewed a large number of five- and six-year-olds about their siblings, and in every aspect of the relationship that the children mentioned the individual differences were huge. Some children said that they played very frequently with their siblings; others rarely did so. Twenty-eight percent said that they quarreled constantly; 36 percent said that they hardly ever quarreled. When asked if they preferred to play with the sibling or a friend, some were adamant that they preferred to play with other children, while others said that they definitely preferred the sibling. Helen Koch asked the children, "Would you be happier without [your sibling]—i.e., if you didn't have a sister or brother? Or do you like it better the way it is, with [your sibling] living at your home? Or doesn't it make any difference to you whether or not you have a sister or brother?"

The questions elicited some striking answers. First, few of the children were indifferent in their response. One third of the children said yes, they'd definitely prefer to be without the sibling. "Yes, I would be happier without her. Could you make her disappear? She bosses me too much." Most, however, were clear that they would rather have the sibling than be without—even if some of them couched the preference in not very complimentary terms: "Oh, I'll keep him. He's bad, but not that bad." The question was an interesting one because in the children's replies they gave in vivid terms their reasons for liking or disliking the sibling. Children who said that they would be happier with the sibling than without frequently showed appreciation for services rendered: "She helps me do coloring." "She buys me things." "My brother always lets me listen to his books." They liked the protection the sibling provided: "He takes me to school." "I wouldn't go to school without her 'cause I'm afraid to." They also commented on personal things about the sibling. Some examples: "I like the way he giggles." "She's little and kind." "He's got soft hair." "She's pretty." "He's cute." Comfort and companionship in play with the sibling were also frequently referred to. The children who said that they would be happier without the sibling emphasized conflict and bossiness and abuse from the brother or sister: "She makes me cry." "He always socks me." "She's so mean sometimes." "He bosses me."

Emotional comments about the sibling were also common in a much more recent study of six-year-olds carried out in Cambridge, England, by Robin Stillwell. She asked the children about their relationships with their friends, their siblings, and their parents, and found that the children used many more emotional terms, both positive and negative, when describing their siblings than they did when talking about any of their other friends or relations. In talking about their siblings they were articulate and expressive and left little doubt about the emotional quality of the relationship. The children used more unfriendly than friendly terms to describe their siblings: their descriptions were primarily couched in negative terms. However, 27 percent of the comments were very positive, and it was the differences between the children in the proportions of these friendly comments that were particularly revealing. While all the children expressed very clearly what it was that they disliked about their sibling, the children who also made friendly and affectionate remarks about the sibling as six-year-olds were the same children who three to four years earlier had been particularly friendly—an issue that we will come back to in chapter 9. Interestingly, Robin Stillwell found good agreement between the children's own accounts of their relationships with their siblings, and the descriptions that their mothers gave of the quality of the sibling relationship. The children who used a high proportion of friendly comments in describing their siblings were reported by their mothers to have very positive relationships with their siblings, relationships with generous sharing and little fighting. In contrast, the children who used a high proportion of negative comments in describing their siblings were said by their mothers to have more ambivalent relationships, in which physical aggression was frequent.

There were some surprises in Helen Koch's study. Comparatively few of the five- and six-year-olds described their sibling as bossy, though there were important differences between firstborn and laterborn siblings here, as we'll see in the next chapter. And half the children said that their sibling never spoiled their toys or games, and reported no problems over possessions. Perhaps most surprisingly (and encouraging for parents), 73 percent of the children said that they would like to have *another* sibling—in spite of all the hostile things they had said about their brother or sister.

Naturally, the kinds of terms that children use to describe their siblings change as they grow up. Children of five tend to describe their siblings in very concrete and self-centered terms: "He hits me when he gets mad." With increasing age, a study by Jerry Bigner showed, they are more likely to use abstract terms about the sibling as a person: "He's very nice and kind." "He's mean." They also begin to comment on a much wider range of aspects of the sibling's personality. Just as Stillwell found that six-year-olds were particularly articulate about the things that they *disliked* about their siblings, so too Bigner found that the more elaborate, sophisticated, and abstract terms were used to describe the *disliked* qualities of the sibling at all ages. Children usually described the qualities that they liked in very concrete terms, and often in terms of the benefits which they themselves accrued as a result: "He tells me neat bedtime stories." In contrast, they began to use more general terms to describe what they didn't like about the sibling.

"He's too unreasonable." "She's too much trouble for everyone." They began to comment in a relatively sophisticated way about the disliked features of the sibling: "Sometimes she wishes I were gone."

There is a parallel here with the findings discussed in Chapter 3—that preschool-aged children can show relatively advanced and mature behavior in conflict with the sibling. The sixteen-month-old who in teasing shows a relatively mature understanding of what will annoy her sibling is not yet very adept as a comforter, or even as a cooperative partner in the more elaborate games her sister tries to establish. With the six- and seven-year-olds, their perceptions about themselves and the others in their family are particularly advanced in relation to the conflict and ambivalence of the sibling relationship. Here are quotations from seven-year-olds who were studied by Carolyn Zahn-Waxler as part of a study of children's understanding of emotions:

> *Mother:* It's hard to hear the baby crying like that.
> *Child:* Yes it is; but it's not as hard for me as it is for you.
> *Mother:* Why?
> *Child:* Well, you like Johnny better than I do! I like him a little and you like him a lot, so I think it's harder for you to hear him cry.

A second child explained to a younger sister why another child had not been responsive to the sister's attempts to comfort her: "Well, that's all right. Sometimes when I hit you and then I want to comfort you, you push me away because you're still angry." These are perceptive and sophisticated comments from a child who is only seven years old. Again we see that within the sibling relationship, children achieve a degree of maturity and understanding that would surprise many psychologists.

It is clear from the interview studies of children five to seven years old that conflict, jealousy, sharing, companionship, and ambivalence between siblings continue as the children grow into middle childhood. The *nature* of siblings' play together obviously changes as they grow up, but one important feature of their companionship remains constant. As John and Elizabeth Newson point out in their study of seven-year-olds, a real advantage of the play between siblings is that in contrast to play with same-aged children, it provides an opportunity to play either protectively and dominatingly or as a follower. While this can obviously also be a disadvantage, it can be a relief and a pleasure to a child to take either role, as this Nottingham mother's description of her seven-year-old suggests: "He plays with Alice [aged two]. He *sometimes* does things with Daniel [aged ten], but the relationship between Alice and himself is of a different type—um . . . he's very good and nice with her, but he's a little bit bossy and teasing, whereas if he plays with Daniel *he's* the one who's bossed. He and Daniel play on Sunday morning and Saturday morning, but they . . . Daniel is very critical of Charles's efforts, and so he tends not to have too much of it."

In some families at least, the sibling relationship remains an intensely important one throughout childhood. Here is a passage—apparently largely autobiographical—which George Eliot wrote for her book *The Mill on the Floss* (she did not include it in the final version). It captures the intensity of affection which little Maggie felt for her older brother Tom, and her longing for his company and affection.

[Maggie] down by the holly made her little world just what she would like it to be . . . Tom never went to school, and liked no one to play with him but Maggie; they went out together somewhere every day, and carried either hot buttered cakes with them because it was baking day, or apple puffs well sugared; Tom was never angry with her for forgetting things, and liked her to tell him tales; there were no bulls to run at her, or fierce dogs chained up and leaping out unexpectedly; her mother never wanted her hair to curl or to have her wear frills that pricked her, and the patchwork was mislaid somewhere, where it could never be found again. Above all Tom loved her—oh so much,—more even than she loved him, so that he would always want to have her with him and be afraid of vexing her; and he as well as everyone else thought her very clever.

Maggie loves her brother passionately. But there is no simple distinction between siblings who get along very well and those who get along badly. Jealousy, for instance, seems to cut right across the other features of the relationship: two siblings who fight rarely and share frequently may be very jealous of each other's relationship with the parents, whereas another pair who are always fighting may not be jealous of parental attention and affection.

Tolstoy in *Anna Karenina* gives us a lovely example of the complexity of the relationship between brothers and sisters—its emotions and dramas—and vividly illuminates the pleasure and the pain felt by the mother who witnesses both the compassion and the hostility the children show one another. Little Tanya supports her brother, Grisha, who has been "unjustly" punished by their governess for a misdemeanor by being denied some tart. Their mother, Darya Alexandrovna, decides to persuade the governess to forgive Grisha, and goes to speak with her.

But on her way, as she passed the drawing-room, she beheld a scene filling her heart with such pleasure that the tears came into her eyes, and she forgave the delinquent herself.

The culprit was sitting at the window in the corner of the drawing-room; beside him was standing Tanya with a plate. On the pretext of wanting to give some dinner to her dolls, she had asked the governess's permission to take her share of tart to the nursery, and had taken it instead to her brother. While still weeping over the injustice of his punishment, he was eating the tart, and kept saying through his sobs, "Eat yourself; let's eat it together . . . together."

Tanya had at first been under the influence of her pity for Grisha, then of a sense of her noble action, and tears were standing in her eyes too; but she did not refuse, and ate her share.

On catching sight of their mother they were dismayed, but, looking into her face, they saw they were not doing wrong. They burst out laughing, and, with their mouths full of tart, they began wiping their smiling lips with their hands, and smearing their radiant faces all over with tears and jam.

"Mercy! Your new white frock; Tanya! Grisha!" said their mother, trying to save the frock, but with tears in her eyes, smiling a blissful, rapturous smile.

Later in the day, however, this pride and happiness in her children is shattered when she sees them fighting:

Grisha and Tanya had been fighting over a ball. Darya Alexandrovna, hearing a scream in the nursery, ran in and saw a terrible sight. Tanya was pulling Grisha's hair, while he, with a face hideous with rage, was beating her with his fists wherever he could get at her. Something snapped in Darya Alexandrovna's heart when she saw this. It was as if darkness had swooped down upon her life; she felt that these children of hers, that she was so proud of, were not merely most ordinary, but positively bad, ill-bred children, with coarse, brutal propensities— wicked children.

She could not talk or think of anything else, and she could not speak to Levin of her misery.

This *combination* of affection and hostility is evident too, with older brothers and sisters. Wyndol Furman interviewed a large number of ten- to thirteen-year-olds about their relations with their sibling, asking them what they thought was important about the relationship. The children talked about affection, comforting, and helping, but also about antagonism and quarreling. And it is striking that these different qualities of the relationship were not closely linked. Children who described their relationship with their brother or sister as very warm, close, and affectionate, for instance, were not necessarily those children who experienced little conflict with the sibling or who expressed little rivalry with each other. And the children who fought a great deal with their siblings were not necessarily the children who reported much jealousy about the parents.

The same story emerges from a study of adolescent siblings who were interviewed to find out to what extent they saw themselves as different from each other, and in what ways. In general, the siblings saw themselves as very different, but there was little connection between the different features of their relationship. Antagonism and conflict were not closely linked to jealousy, or to the degree of closeness the siblings felt, or to the relative dominance of the adolescents.

WATCHING BROTHERS AND SISTERS

Children talking about their siblings, then, refer to the affection and support, the conflict and fights, the dominance and rivalry between them. What can we learn from *watching* what brothers and sisters of this age range do together? Very few people have attempted to study siblings older than six by observing them directly. The problems are obviously very great. An observer lurking around the house will hardly be ignored by six- to ten-year-olds. The children will be all too well aware of what he or she is up to. In the 1930s Charlotte Bühler in Vienna tackled the problem of observing the behavior of such sophisticated and self-aware children by training observers carefully to watch and record the children's interactions, not in a laboratory setup but while they were full participants in the children's family life. They visited the homes twice a week for three to six months, and there was no attempt to make these observers "flies on the wall." Rather, they became friends of the families and were treated in a very relaxed way by the family members. This study yielded detailed systematic observations of a very few families. Although the results are limited in scope, they are valuable because they stand so alone in studies of siblings of this age range, and because in certain ways they bring out strongly the same themes that emerged from the observations of very young siblings.

One theme, not apparent from most interview studies, is that the siblings spent a great deal of time in activities that were *imitative*. Sometimes the children were *acting together* at the same time, with a close meshing of their interests. Sometimes the imitations were what Charlotte Bühler called "successive": one child would immediately copy what the other child had just done. She stressed that some of these "mutual imitations" reflected the competition and rivalry between the siblings, especially the successive imitations. One child would repeat the other's action to show that he or she could do it as well— or better. But this was by no means always the case. The sequences of imitations, she argued, frequently expressed the close unity of the children's lives and interests. The frequency of the imitations was very high: 33 percent of the children's actions together were simultaneous imitations, and 21 percent were successive imitations.

There is a striking parallel between these observations of children aged four to thirteen years and the observations of imitations between preschool-aged children and their baby brothers and sisters. It brings out clearly the salience of the sibling for children—even for such relatively "grown-up" children.

Cooperation was another theme that stood out from Charlotte Bühler's observations. Giving each other toys, doing things for each other, taking each other's part— all these were common between the children. Hostility and antagonism, too, were frequent. Among the middle-class Viennese children Bühler was studying, these feelings were not usually expressed physically. But ridicule and sarcasm, belittling the sibling, and asserting one's own importance were all very frequent. Here are some examples from the observations of two sisters, Käthe (six) and Erna (ten):

Erna had a constant desire to elevate herself above Käthe and to belittle her younger sister. She knew how to subdue her and make her accomplishments appear insignificant by means of a multitude of nasty remarks.

Mother is telling the observer that Käthe would not enjoy being at the lake because she cannot swim. Käthe claims that she knows how, but Erna says: "Go on, you can't at all, and you haven't even begun to learn. You've only been in once."

Käthe: "No, three times."

Erna: "Well, anyway, you don't know how, and you can't sew either."

While the girls are doing their school work, Erna says: "Käthe thinks that 1,000 plus 1,000 equals a million."

Käthe protests that she said 2,000. Erna insists and calls Käthe stupid.

Käthe runs and skips around. Erna says deprecatingly: "You can't even jump."

Käthe continues to run.

Erna continues: "I can jump two feet."

She proceeds to make remarks about her sister's running and jumping.

When their father wants to take a picture of the children and the observer, Erna assumes a graceful position, saying: "I can stand this way because I am big, but Käthe can't."

On the same occasion, Erna admonishes Käthe: "Now don't make such a dumb face as you usually do."

Käthe: "But I don't make dumb faces."

Erna: "You do, too; mother said so herself."

Even the brothers and sisters who got along well in Charlotte Bühler's studies did not praise each other's achievements before the age of seven, and only rarely did so before the age of nine.

The detailed observations of the siblings made another important point very clear. Not only were the individual differences between the sibling pairs very marked—with some pairs cooperative, affectionate, and warm, and others full of antagonism and conflict—but the behavior of two siblings within the same family could be dramatically and consistently different. One child would be systematically hostile, disparaging, and un-friendly, while her sister submitted in a neutral way to the unending unpleasantness and even made friendly overtures which were always ignored. The parallel here with the "mismatch" observed between preschool-aged siblings is important. It is evidence that chil-dren *can* make the same family environment very dif-ferent for each other, and thus may directly contribute to the development of individual differences between siblings.

Two other points are illustrated by Bühler's study. First, the parents' involvement with the children was crucially important to an understanding of the relation-ship between the siblings. Parents were involved in a very high proportion of the exchanges between the chil-dren, especially the antagonistic exchanges, and the warmth and affection of the parent-child relationship seemed to be centrally important as an influence on the siblings' relationship. Second, the birth order of the chil-dren and their sexes did not appear to explain the dif-ferences in their relationships. In the next two chapters we take up these points, and come to very much the same conclusion as Charlotte Bühler.

ROLES WITHIN THE FAMILY

It is often said that the different children in a family take on different roles in relation to the other family members—roles recognized by themselves, by their brothers and sisters, and by the parents. One child will be characterized as the "outgoing, cheerful, social" one;

another as the "rebel"; another as the "responsible" one. There is no good evidence showing how often or how consistently siblings are characterized in this way, or what the consequences for their development might be. In a study of large families, James Bossard and Eleanor Boll found that brothers and sisters growing up in a group of six or more other children *did* develop particular roles. In large families, much of this role assignment seemed to be done by the siblings themselves. The most frequently cited role was that of the "responsible" one. This was usually the firstborn, who in these large families tended to take on major responsibilities: "The word 'responsible' is the one used most frequently in referring to these siblings, but in some cases such words as 'dutiful,' 'bossy,' 'drudge,' 'leader,' 'helpful,' 'martinet,' and 'policeman' are also used. These seem to identify chiefly the way in which this position of responsibility was exercised." The second most frequently quoted role was the "popular, social sibling":

Second son. He has developed the most normal personality of all of us. He is best liked by our parents and by the other children.

Second daughter. The attractive one. Most popular one among all of us. Interested in the personal appearance of all of us. She would wash your hair and fix you up to go out if mother was busy.

Second son. He was the one with *the* personality. He was much admired by all of us.

Second son. Everybody likes him. He is very sociable. He gets along well with everyone. He is good-looking, and always knows the right thing to say and do and wear.

Other roles mentioned were the "socially ambitious one," the "studious one," the "protected, babied one."

Although we don't know how realistic these categorizations are, or how frequently they occur in smaller families, it's worth considering the questions which such role assignments raise. First, it is clear that as children grow up in the school years the possibilities for assigning a child to a particular role increase. For instance, as a child's mathematical talents become clear, everyone in the family becomes more conscious both of his talent and of the differences in this respect between him and his brothers and sisters. A second example is the responsible role. As a first child reaches middle childhood he is likely to be given more responsibilities for looking after his younger siblings, and this role in a very practical sense becomes one that he is repeatedly encouraged to take on. Again, the differences between him and his siblings become more clearly delineated as the children grow up. This suggests one process which may contribute to the marked differences between siblings. There is some evidence (as we'll see in Chapter 8) that the differences between children brought up within the same family become *more* extreme as the children reach middle childhood and adolescence, and this assignation of roles could indeed be one way in which the differences become more marked in the shool years.

The second issue is also a developmental one. What does it mean to be characterized as the "social, popular one," in a family? Or the "anxious sensitive one?" Is it a self-fulfilling prophecy? How does it affect a child's conception of himself? After the early years of childhood, differences in children's senses of self-esteem become evident. The question of how a child's sense of himself in relation to his siblings affects his self-confidence more generally is an important one.

THE WORLD OUTSIDE THE FAMILY

How do the different aspects of the relationship between brothers and sisters affect their behavior in the world outside home—their relationships with friends and school companions? Does the relationship between a child and his or her sibling influence his sense of self-esteem, and his growing sense of how others view him? If he grows from four years to ten years old with someone who knows him intimately, spends a great deal of time with him, and relentlessly disparages and criticizes him while appearing effortlessly more capable and successful, surely this experience will have a profound effect on his sense of his own value and efficacy, and will affect his behavior with others outside the home.

Here is Tolstoy, writing about "my elder brother" Volodya in his (largely autobiographical) book *Childhood, Boyhood, and Youth.*

> I was only a year and some months younger than Volodya; we grew up, studied and played together. No distinction of elder and younger was made between us; but just about the time I am speaking of I began to realize that I was no companion for him, either in age, in interests or in ability. It even seemed to me that Volodya himself was aware of his superiority and was proud of it. This idea (it may have been a wrong one) was inspired by my vanity—which suffered every time I came in contact with him. He was better than I in everything: at games, at lessons, in arguments and in manners, and all this estranged me from him and occasioned me moral anguish which I could not understand. If I had said frankly when Volodya was given tucked linen shirts for the first time that I was vexed at not having shirts like that, I am sure I should have felt happier and not thought

every time he arranged his collar that it was only done to annoy me.

What tormented me most was that it sometimes seemed to me Volodya understood what was going on inside me but tried to hide this . . . I could not help being enticed by his hobbies but I was too proud to imitate him and too young and not independent enough to choose a line for myself. But there was nothing I envied so much as Volodya's happy big-hearted disposition, which showed itself most strikingly when we quarreled. I always felt that he was behaving well but I could not do likewise.

We don't as yet have much evidence that there is a clear or consistent connection between the quality of a child's relationship with his siblings, his sense of self-esteem, and his behavior in the world of school and friends. Robin Stillwell found that children who were very jealous of their siblings—according to their mother's reports—had low self-esteem. However, this link did not show up in the children's own reports of their relationship with their siblings, and in any case it is impossible to decide on the direction of the causal link here. It could be that children who have low self-esteem tend to watch and mind more about their siblings' accomplishments and relationships with the parents, or it could be that the jealous relationship between the children increases an already vulnerable child's low opinion of himself. It is clearly an area in which psychologists should do more extensive research. It is possible, of course, that it is a child's relationship with his *peers* that is most crucial to his sense of self-esteem, and that by the time a child enters school any belittling or undermining influence of his sibling is less important than how his own school friends view him.

What of the possible links between a child's experiences with the sibling and his behavior with these all-important peers at school? Again we don't have clear or extensive evidence on the issue. Stillwell's study of six-year-olds found little connection between the children's friendship patterns at school and the quality of their sibling relationship. According to their mothers, children who shared happily with their siblings were happy and generous in sharing with their friends. There was a suggestion, too, that children who had very aggressive relationships with their siblings were also aggressive with their peers. But the connections were not strong or consistent. How children get along with peers is clearly influenced by a great many factors: their personalities, their relations with their parents, and the social world of the school, as well as their experiences with their siblings. So it is hardly surprising that we don't find a simple link between the relationships children have with their siblings and with friends.

The experience of growing up with close and affectionate siblings could, of course, affect a child's behavior with peers in very different ways. It could be that if a child has a very intense, intimate, and companionable sibling relationship, then friends are less important and less sought after, and the child has less opportunity to develop the social skills involved in establishing friendships with unfamiliar children. Or conversely, a childhood spent in a lively, friendly family of brothers and sisters could give a child great confidence and social ease with other children.

Which of these alternatives is the most plausible? The results of Bossard and Boll's study suggest that the former certainly can happen. Several of the people interviewed who had grown up with lots of brothers and sisters, especially those from isolated rural communities, stressed that while the close world of the large family had great advantages it also led to difficulties in making friends outside the family.

> We lived within our group, and did not become as well prepared to cope with the outside world as does the only child whose parents seek contacts for it with the outside world. We were not shy within the group. One child attended church with her mother when she was seven years old, and for the first three Sundays she attended she was terrified of the strange people and wept hysterically whenever anyone spoke to her. If she had had the familiar presence of one of her brothers to gather comfort from, this outside contact doubtless would not have been so painful. After three Sundays of tears she gathered up her courage to look around and to discover the people weren't nearly as alarming as she had fancied. But she still felt unsure and alone, away from the safety and comfort of the group . . . Some of us, even as adults, have not outgrown the sense of fear and insecurity we felt on being exposed to outside contacts, and in one or two cases has developed to such an extent that the feeling has become a sort of inferiority complex.
>
> On the negative side, children in large families tend to lose contacts on the outside. The family life becomes a complete social world. There is no reaching out into other homes. This is particularly true of an isolated farm family.
>
> There is a danger that a large family will provide a sheltered adjustment that will monopolize a child's life and keep it from facing the more difficult adjustments that must be made outside of the home. I may not have retreated into the sheltered life of my own home, but neither did I gain sufficient experience in socializing myself for life outside.

These quotes come from a retrospective study in which adults drew on their memories of childhood. We still know very little from more direct research about how the sibling relationship affects the way a child develops and feels about himself in the middle childhood years.

In the preschool years, as we saw, both play and conflict between siblings highlight the children's powers of understanding each other, and both also provide particularly important contexts in which children grow to understand the social rules and roles of their world. In the middle years of childhood, play and argument are probably just as important. Jean Piaget believed that discussions and arguments between children are of special significance in moral development. He suggested that because children share more equal status with each other than they do with adults, when they have to arbitrate the way in which games are to be played and to resolve conflicts without recourse to adults they learn to understand both the perspective of the other child and the meaning and function of social rules. If this hypothesis is valid (and it sounds plausible, even though it has not yet been tested), then the play and conflicts of siblings who are both very familiar and emotionally engaged with each other should be particularly important in the development of social understanding in the middle childhood years.

The importance of siblings in the development of moral and social judgments was also stressed by Anna Freud, a clinician whose wise comments on children were based on a very different background and experience from those of Piaget: "The child's first approach to the idea of justice is made during these developments of the brother-sister relationship, when the claim to be favoured oneself is changed to the demand that no one should be favoured, i.e. that there should be equal rights for everybody. Since contemporaries outside the family are treated like the siblings, these first relationships to the brothers and sisters become important factors in determining the individual's social attitudes." Sigmund Freud, too, said that the origins of a sense of justice lay in the relationship between brothers and sisters: "The elder child illtreats the younger, maligns him and robs him of his toys; while the younger is consumed with impotent rage against the elder, envies and fears him, or meets his oppressor with the first stirrings of a love of liberty and a sense of justice." Loyalty, he argued, also grew out of the sibling relationship:

> For a long time nothing in the nature of herd instinct or group feeling is observed in children. Something like it first grows up, in nurseries containing many children, out of the children's relation to the parents, and it does so as a reaction to the initial envy with which the elder child receives the younger one. The elder child would certainly like to put his successor jealously aside, to keep it away from the parents, and to rob it of all its privileges; but in face of the fact that this younger child (like all that come later) is loved by the parents as much as he himself is, and in consequence of the impossibility of his maintaining his hostile attitude without damaging himself, he is forced to identify himself with the other children. So there grows up in the troop of children a communal or group feeling.

Freud believed that the rivalry between siblings for their parents' love is the origin even of their loyalty to one another. This emphasis on competition between siblings for parental love as the *only* dimension of importance in their relationship does appear to be misleading, in the light of the recent observational studies discussed earlier. However, think for a moment of the issues that dominate the arguments and discussions of siblings and their parents: equity—the fairness with which parents treat their different children, the fairness with which "scarce" resources are distributed (usually which TV program should be watched); possession, sharing, and rules; who is allowed to do what. Anna Freud is surely right to stress the importance of these family discussions of rights, rules, and moral obligations in the formation of children's attitudes. And arguments *between* siblings are central to such discussions. Think, too, of the importance that children attribute to loyalty, protection, and support between siblings when they face other children and hostile or disparging peers. The importance of these qualities in a sibling were stressed even by children as young as five years, as seen in Helen Koch's study.

The views of children on their siblings and the observations of their relationship during the early school years illuminate in a number of ways the issues of sibling influence and the development of social understanding. It is clear that the relationship between school-aged siblings continues to be one of emotional power for many children, and is thus potentially an important developmental influence. The distinctive features of the early years which support the case for sibling influence—the frequent imitation, the mismatch interactions, the uninhibited emotional quality of their exchanges—continue to be evident. And it seems likely that as they grow up, siblings increasingly take on different roles within the family—an indirect effect of the sibling's presence upon the child's developing personality. Processes of comparison with the sibling are also likely to be a powerful influence on children, though evidence for these remains scanty. With regard to our third theme—the sibling relationship as a context in which children's powers of social understanding are vividly revealed and fostered—the early school years are particularly interesting. Childen talk about their siblings, for instance, in a relatively sophisticated way and in more emotional terms than they use to comment on other people. It seems plausible too, that disputes with siblings over issues of social rules and moral obligations are important in the formation of children's attitudes to social rules, as well as in the development of their skills of argument. But in spite of these hypotheses about the importance of siblings throughout childhood, our *knowledge* about what happens between them during the childhood years is pitifully scanty, and confined to Western culture. Psychologists are only just beginning to include siblings in their attempts to answer the question of why children develop different personalities and capabilities. But we know from the writing of novelists and poets, from autobiographies and letters, just how much importance many adults have given their childhood experiences with their brothers and sisters. The extent to which writers such as the Brontës, Tolstoy, and George Eliot drew directly on their own experiences with their brothers and sisters, and the importance of these experiences in their imaginative life, are vividly captured in their novels. Psychologists, in contrast, have hardly begun to examine the influence of family experiences in the middle childhood years on children's sense of themselves, their personalities, and their intellectual and imaginative abilities, although it is clear that individual differences between sibling pairs continue to be very marked in the early school years. Psychologists have not focused on the impact of different kinds of sibling relationships—affectionate, conflict-ridden, jealous, domineering. Instead, they have made numerous attempts to establish to what extent birth order, sex of sibling, and the age gap between siblings affect children. The next chapter deals with these issues.

5 / Birth Order, Age Gap, Gender, and Large Families

In some families the children constantly fight with and irritate each other; in others they offer each other affectionate support that is moving to see. Compare the following comments by two mothers, each with a three-year-old and a fourteen-month-old:

> He gets into everything of hers. It drives her crazy. They fight such a lot—screaming quarrels. And it's not just screaming—they really go at each other.

> He [the younger sibling] loves being with her and her friends . . . He trails after Laura . . . they play in the sand a lot . . . making pies. She organizes it and whisks away things that are dangerous and gives him something else. They go upstairs and bounce on the bed. Then he'll lie there while she sings to him and reads books to him. And he'll go off in a trance with his hankie [comfort object]. The important thing is they're becoming games that they'll play together. He'll start something by laughing and running toward some toy, turning round to see if she's following. He'll go upstairs and race into the bedroom and shriek, and she joins him.

What could explain these differences in how the children get along together and in what they feel for each other? Books for parents frequently imply that jealousy and quarrels between siblings are largely the fault of the parents. But it is also often said that a child's birth order, the age difference between her and her siblings, and their sexes all influence how well they get along. How much evidence is there to support these views?

FIRSTBORNS AND LATERBORNS

It certainly seems plausible that firstborn children should feel more hostility toward siblings than is felt by laterborns. The firstborn children are, after all, the ones who have been displaced. As one mother said of her two-year-old's feelings about her younger brother, the secondborn: "She was queen of the world . . . no wonder she minds and seems to resent him." And as a precocious four-year-old put it quite explicitly to his mother on the birth of his brother: "Why have you ruined my life?"

It will not surprise any parent who has more than one child to hear that firstborn children tend to express more ambivalence and hostility about their siblings than vice versa. Both firstborns and laterborns believe that the parents align themselves with the younger siblings rather than with the eldest. This remark by a five-year-old girl in Helen Koch's study is not an unusual comment from a firstborn child: "Yes, I would like to change places with my baby brother. Then I could yell my head off and my mommy would take care of nobody but me."

Firstborns are less likely to say that they prefer to play with their siblings than with other children. They are seen by both first- and laterborn children as bossier and more dominant than laterborn children, and studies of five- and six-year-olds show that their power tactics in dealing with their siblings tend to differ. Here is a firstborn boy describing how he gets his sister to do what he wants: "I told her to get out of my room. And I kept shouting at her and she wouldn't go. And I started hitting her, and she still wouldn't go. So I just picked her up and threw her out."

According to a study of siblings' power tactics by Brian Sutton-Smith, firstborn children attack, use status more, and bribe. Laterborns tend to sulk, pout, plead, cry, and appeal to parents for help. The more polite techniques of explaining, taking turns, and asking are perceived by most children as the strategies only of firstborn girls. Sutton-Smith and his colleagues offer the following interpretation of these differences. The status tactics, bossiness, and dominance of firstborns are typical of the powerful members of any social system—those who are larger and have greater ability; the appeals of laterborn children to their parents for support are typical of the weak members of social groups and are encouraged by the greater indulgence and comfort offered to laterborn children by their parents (see Chapter 6). The tendency of firstborn girls to explain and give reasons reflects the way in which the girls model themselves on their mother, with whom (it is assumed) they have closer relations than do the secondborn girls. Sutton-Smith's account sounds plausible, but it is probably far too simple, and we simply don't have evidence to support some of the arguments. For instance, there's no good evidence that secondborn girls have a less close relationship with their mothers than firstborn girls.

During their early years, laterborn children are frequently more directly aggressive than their older siblings, according to the interview studies. They may not be any more hostile—but they do express their aggression very directly and physically. Firstborns tend to be more *verbally* aggressive, criticizing and disparaging their younger brothers and sisters mercilessly. This "childs-eye" view of firstborns as bossy and dominant is supported by experiments in which siblings are asked to play or carry out tasks together. Seven- and eight-year-old firstborns are in these situations more likely to dominate, to praise, and to teach their siblings than vice versa.

Of course, it is not always the eldest who is the dominating one. When competition or domination comes from a younger sibling it can be particularly devastating for the older sibling. Here are the comments of a Nottingham mother, in the Newsons' study, describing her seven-year-old's reaction to a very bright younger sibling:

> He's not afraid of anything physical—his fears are attached to not being able to understand. He's said once or twice something that rather horrified me: "I don't understand; there must be something the matter with me." This is the business of his relationship with Katherine [aged five-and-a-half]. It's just simply that James is not so intelligent as Katherine, and he's cottoning on to this fact very quickly, and I don't know what to do about it. [Has he been conscious of it for some time?] I think so—since Katherine started going to school and came home with reports of what she'd done, what book they were reading. His initial response was "You couldn't have done"; and she said "We did" and proceeded to show him. He was absolutely devastated.

What is so poignant here is the awareness of both child and mother that this is not a problem that will disappear, but one that will have to be lived with, for a lifetime.

Firstborn children from large families, especially, often have a particular role as disciplinarians, caregivers, and leaders. The study by James Bossard and Eleanor Boll includes many vivid examples of the responsibilities placed on firstborn children. The adults recalling these experiences felt that they had important consequences for their development. These are the recollections of the oldest daughter in a family with nine children:

For as long as I can remember, I helped with the dishes and then was given the responsibility of other tasks as I grew older . . . There were eleven of us eating every day. Life seemed to be one eternity of dirty dishes after another . . . It was my job to make the chocolate cupcakes for five school lunches that were carried, pack the lunches, and set the table for breakfast. I was in disgrace with my brothers and sisters if I failed to get up in time to make the cakes and I was too poor a baker to make them good enough to be edible the next day. I learned to bake bread and to iron before I was in high school. I have a faint recollection of washing, feeding, and caring for the baby when I was seven years old. I was "mother's little helper" in so many ways for years. Mother certainly needed me. When we went visiting, it was my responsibility to see that the younger children did no damage or did not get hurt. My household tasks gradually increased until I was doing more of it than mother was. Her last baby was born at the beginning of Christmas vacation of my last year in high school, and I was put into complete charge, including mother and the baby. Being the oldest girl in a large family meant that many of my own desires remained unfulfilled.

And here are the comments of the oldest of eight:

From the time that I was five, I can remember taking care of the children. I used to lie on my mother's bed and push my little brother back and forth in his carriage until he fell asleep. Mother kept on having babies. Many problems beset us. By the time I was in third grade, I was always helping mother while the others played with the neighboring children. This made me old beyond my years, serious, and quite responsible for all that went on in the household . . . Each Saturday, my mother went in to the city six miles away for the groceries and stayed for the day. In the evening she and dad visited friends and came home at about midnight. From age fifteen to nineteen, I found myself responsible for seeing that the housework was finished, cooking lunch and dinner for the children, and caring for the newest baby. At night, I bathed six children, washed their heads, and tucked them into bed. Saturday nights continued like this until I rebelled. I wanted to have time for dates like other girls had.

In contrast, if we look at siblings in smaller families and take account of individual differences in affection, warmth, aggression, and conflict between siblings, it is surprising how unimportant birth order per se turns out to be. Although power and dominance between siblings are closely related to birth order, these other features of the relationship are *not*. The closeness, intimacy, support, and affection a child feels for his brother or sister is not clearly linked to whether he is a firstborn or laterborn, and it is these features of the sibling relationship that are likely to be of particular importance in the influence of siblings upon one another.

The interview and questionnaire studies of children between the ages of six and twelve suggest that the sex and personality of the firstborn child are more likely to influence the secondborn than vice versa, at least in terms of gender role, interests, and activities. Firstborns, in comparison, are more likely to be influenced by their parents. In families with very young children, as we saw in Chapter 2, laterborn children imitate their older siblings far more than their older siblings imitate them—

at least after the first year of life. It is likely, then, that laterborn children model themselves on their older siblings much more than the other way around. But we should not jump to the simple conclusion that whereas laterborns are influenced by their older siblings, firstborns are not influenced by their younger siblings. This is an oversimplification that masks a very complex pattern of mutual influences between siblings and their parents. However, the first child's feelings about the sibling, and his or her behavior toward the sibling in the first years, are of quite special significance as an influence on the way their relationship develops. In one Cambridge study, firstborn children were observed over many months, beginning before the birth of the second child. In families where the first child showed marked affectionate interest in the newborn, the younger child was likely to be particularly friendly to the elder one year later. In these families the firstborns, by their initial interest in the baby sibling, set up a relationship of affection that continued for several years to be very friendly. The differences in the firstborn children's response to the birth were, then, very important in accounting for differences in the relationship which developed between the first two children in the family.

What could explain these differences between firstborn children in their behavior toward the new sibling? One key factor was the nature of the parents' relationship with the first child before and immediately after the sibling's birth. Another was the firstborn's temperament. Children who were anxious, "withdrawing" individuals before the birth usually had little interest in or affection for the new sibling. However, the age gap between the children was *not* related to their interest in the baby. Among the most affectionately interested were some very young children—only eighteen to nineteen months old—and some three- to four-year-olds. And there were no differences between the boys and girls in the sample in how interested they were in the baby sibling.

Follow-up observations of these siblings showed just how important the first child's feelings about the baby were as an influence on their developing relationship. However, it is also likely that differences in the second-born's behavior toward the first, even in the first eighteen months of life, affect how the older child feels about the second. Michael Lamb studied pairs of siblings when the secondborn was twelve months old, and then again six months later. He found that the behavior of the first children toward their siblings was predicted *better* by the behavior of the secondborn infants at the first visits than it was by the firstborn children's own behavior at those first visits. The more sociable the babies were at the first session, the more sociable their older siblings were toward them at the second visit.

We just do not know, with children older than pre-schoolers, whether differences in the behavior of the first- and laterborn siblings influence the way in which the relationship between the children develops. This is partly because most studies have looked only at the sex of and age gap between the siblings and not at the individual differences in affection or hostility. It has been assumed that it is the sex of the children and the age gap between them that are of the most significance. But do boys and girls differ in the way they behave toward their siblings?

SEX DIFFERENCES

It's often said that a boy growing up with several sisters will be "feminine" in his interests and a girl with brothers will be a "tomboy." In the 1950s and 1960s several psychologists looked at the relation between the extent to which children and adolescents were "masculine" or "feminine" in their interests, occupations, and games, and whether they had grown up with brothers or sisters. The results were complicated, and in some ways contradictory. Laterborn children with an older sibling of the same sex did tend to be the most "stereotypically sex typed." A secondborn boy with an older brother was likely to be very "masculine" in his interests, and girls with older sisters were likely to be particularly "feminine" in theirs.

But the picture is not a simple or a consistent one. For instance, some studies suggested that boys with *two* older sisters showed *less* interest in "feminine" games and occupations, and interacted less with girls in the classroom than did boys with brothers. In explaining these results it was argued that whereas some children "identified" with their siblings, imitated them, and modeled their behavior on them, other children reacted against their siblings by developing very different interests and opposing styles.

It is clear that we could "explain" any particular combination of personalities and interests among the brothers and sisters within a family by referring to these two processes of "identification" and its opposite, "deidentification." Certainly we cannot predict with any confidence the personality or behavior of a child simply on the basis of knowing his or her sex and the sex of the other children in the family.

There are no clear or consistent differences between very young boys and girls in the ways that they behave toward their siblings. For instance, it is sometimes assumed that older sisters are more likely to be nurturant—"little mothers"—than older brothers. But in the cross-cultural studies of John and Beatrice Whiting, in which sibling caregiving by both girls and boys was very common, no sex differences were found in the behavior of the older siblings, although the younger siblings asked for help, comfort, and security from older sisters more frequently than from older brothers.

Sisters are sometimes said to be better teachers than brothers. Boys and girls do have rather different teaching styles. Rob Stewart asked a number of children between the ages of four and five to teach their two-year-old siblings how to use a camera. The best teachers were boys with younger brothers, especially those who were relatively advanced in understanding how to take the perspective of another person. In contrast, Victor Cicirelli found that sisters were more effective teachers than brothers: they used a deductive method more than boys, they offered help more often, and their help was more likely to be accepted.

However, children with an older brother appeared to do better when working alone than children with an older sister. Cicirelli suggests that this may be because a child with an older brother is stimulated by the competition and rivalry of an older brother to learn more than from an older sister, but that in a more formal teaching situation the younger child will learn more from an older sister because she expects to give help and the younger expects to receive it.

In contrast to these results from experimental studies, no sex differences in frequency of teaching by older siblings, or in acceptance of teaching by their younger siblings, have yet been found in studies of children at home.

The same contradictions appear when same-sex and different-sex pairs are compared. With very young siblings there is often a greater amount of friendly, helpful interaction and imitation in same-sex pairs. But in Rob Stewart's study, in which sibling pairs were left alone in a laboratory playroom, the older siblings who were *least* likely to comfort and support their younger siblings were brothers in two-boy families. And among older children, aggression and dominance were more often evident in same-sex pairs: mothers of six-year-olds in the Cambridge studies reported more jealousy in same-sex pairs, for instance. Yet in Helen Koch's extensive interviews, more six-year-olds with same-sex siblings than with different-sex siblings said that they would prefer to play with their sibling rather than with a friend, and more said that they liked looking after their sibling. It was very rare, among Koch's six-year-olds, for a child who had a same-sex sibling to say that he or she would be happier without the sibling.

Why should there be such contradictory results? The different cultural backgrounds of the families studied, the different ages of the children, differences in the way in which the children were studied—all of these factors could contribute to the inconsistencies. But clearly, sex differences in either younger or older siblings *cannot* be linked in a simple or powerfully predictive way to differences in the way the children relate to one another.

AGE DIFFERENCES

People often hold even stronger views on the importance of the age gap between siblings than on the significance of the sex of siblings. Some parents attribute the intimacy and friendliness of their children to their closeness in age. The close matching of interest and effectiveness as partners in play of children who are only two years apart is held to be of real importance. Other parents believe that their children get along well because there is a large age gap between them. The older child, they argue, does not feel so displaced, and since he's more secure is more friendly toward the younger. Both accounts sound plausible, and we can find evidence to support either point of view. With preschool-aged children, the age gap does not appear to be nearly as important as physicians and psychiatrists have supposed. The ways in which firstborns react to the arrival of a sibling do differ with age: fifteen-month-olds tend to react by becoming miserable and clinging, whereas three- to four-year-olds often become very difficult and demanding. But the age difference does not appear to affect the positive interest in the new baby, or the incidence of marked disturbance (see Chapter 7), or the quality of the relationship between the two children as they grow up. Play, companionship, and affection are as frequently shown whether the age gap is four years or only eleven months; so too are aggression, hostility, and teasing.

The more "parent-like" behaviors of teaching and care-giving are more frequently shown by the older children in families in which there is a large age gap. But in many studies the larger the age gap between the children, the greater the age of the older child, and it is hardly surprising that with increasing age children are more effective teachers or caregivers.

With children aged six, seven, and eight, the story is rather different. Helen Koch found that if the gap between the children was between two and four years, all the effects she described—modeling, rivalry, competition—were heightened. With a larger age gap the children played less together, but the laterborns accepted teaching from their older siblings more often and more willingly. In general, the age gap between siblings seems to be more important with six- to eight-year-olds than it is with little children, but there are still many inconsistencies in the findings of different studies. For instance, one study compared seven- and eight-year-olds as they played with their siblings in a competitive game, and as they wrapped a very large box together. If the seven- and eight-year-olds had a sibling close in age (with only one to two years between them), they were more aggressive and less likely to be friendly than if the age gap was three to four years. In contrast, Helen Koch found that siblings who were more than two years apart in age had more competitive and stressful relationships. These contradictions show that we clearly should not draw simple conclusions about the significance (or the insignificance) of the age gap between sisters and brothers.

GROWING UP IN A LARGE FAMILY

Until now, I have talked about the relationship between brothers and sisters mostly in terms of *pairs* of siblings. How different is the experience of growing up with lots of brothers and sisters? The focus on two-children families reflects both the kind of studies that have been done by psychologists and the typical families of Western Europe and the United States. The study of large families conducted by Bossard and Boll in the 1950s gives a different picture of family life. They interviewed and collected written life histories from over 150 people from families with more than six children. It was a retrospective study, drawing on people's recollections and reflections on their childhood experiences, rather than a direct study of the children themselves. It was also not a formal, systematic study. But the insights it gives us are interesting, and balance the picture of brothers and sisters given by studies of smaller families.

First, for many of the children in those large families

there was an important closed world of play with their brothers and sisters: "We rarely had outside company and did not feel the need of it. We had good imaginations and played many games, which were joined in by two dogs and a cat. This life continued for some years, and, as far as we children were concerned, it was the closest thing to heaven." As we saw in the last chapter, some children felt that this closed family world limited their ability to relate to others. Most children, however, felt that living in a large family had very important and useful consequences: learning to share, to develop self-control, and to show consideration for others were repeatedly mentioned. The following three quotations are typical of the views of people from large families:

> Living in a large family socializes a child to an appreciable extent . . . In general, living and being reared in a large family teaches one that life is not a "bed of roses" and that there are other people in the world all with "equal rights" to the pursuit of happiness in life . . . a child in a large family has brothers and sisters of contemporary age who understand him as a child and in the "give and take" of their everyday life each learns to control emotions, think in terms of "we" and not "me," "to live and let live," to look out for oneself and yet to consider the rights of others, and a host of similar terms all meaning to live as a real human being should and not as an animal.

> I think that large family life teaches self-control and self-discipline. When you have three or four or more brothers and sisters who aggravate you in various ways at various times, you soon learn that it is not considered good conduct to grab, shake or strike your brothers and sisters. You learn to control those nasty anti-social acts, or carry their problems to the impartial courts of the law, I don't know. You learn to discipline yourself in many

ways, and to govern your conduct along acceptable social ways . . . I think that being part of a large family
establishes the desire to belong or to be needed. It makes
you like to love and be loved; a large family does not
tend to produce cold, aloof, withdrawn people. It teaches
respect for private property, and consideration for each
other. It produces the desire to help each other or to
guide each other.

Yes, I do honestly believe that living in a large family
does have its effect on socialization because consideration must be given to each other during the course of
living together. A form of unity develops and with it a
sense of attachment for each other. Though privacy is
at a minimum, or rather impossible, one does gain some-
what of a group spirit which implies thinking through
things together and arriving at decisions that are reasonably acceptable to all. I am convinced that a much
more charitable consideration for "the other person" is
engendered by a person who derives from a large family
than one who is a product of a small family.

A second point is that siblings in large families often
have special roles as disciplinarians of their younger
siblings; this rarely happens in two-child or three-child
families. Earlier in this chapter I quoted the words of
one firstborn who had to assume many responsibilities.
How do younger siblings feel about the discipline meted
out by their older siblings? The quotations show that in
many ways sibling discipline can work very well, from
the children's point of view. First, the siblings in the
study did feel that they understood each other and each
other's problems—often better than the parents. Second, they felt that they often had better judgment than
the parents as to what should be considered misbehav-
ior. According to them, this meant that discipline imposed by siblings was often more reasonable, and had

more meaning, than discipline by parents. Third, and most important, they suggested that sibling discipline was more effective than adult discipline because the disapproval of siblings mattered so much more than the disapproval of adults. And as Bossard and Boll comment: "Siblings know what kinds of discipline are effective. They know that a sound spanking, while it may hurt for the time being, may have far less meaning than not being allowed to go fishing with the others. It may be argued here that children are often very cruel to each other, and this certainly is true. Perhaps the real reason for this is not what adults assume it to be, but because children are realists. They know what matters, and what hurts."

The security provided by siblings was stressed by a surprisingly large number of the people from large families—surprisingly, because according to conventional psychiatric wisdom, security for a child is based on the parent-child (and usually the mother-child) relationship. I have commented on the security that even pre-school-aged and infant siblings apparently provide for each other. Here is a parallel emphasis on the security that siblings can provide much later in childhood.

Why should living with a large number of siblings lead to a sense of emotional security? Several reasons were given. One was that within the large family, dependability was highly appreciated, even fostered, in the face of the many hardships with which the family had to cope.

> We did feel a sense of security that must be lacking in small families, because we were required to work together and to the well-being of all of us. This feeling remains—even in our adult years.

We have the philosophy that if we stick together we can get through any crisis. If we stand alone, it makes a hardship on the family . . . Fear with us was unknown, probably because we never stood completely alone.

Emotionally there was strength in being a member of a large family. A crisis was met by everyone and to back up an individual there was a whole clan.

It was also stressed that within the group of siblings there was likely to be at least one person with whom a child could pair up, and who would provide support: "We always had at least one other family member to play with. In smaller families, if you are feuding with your only brother or sister, you would be quite lonely. One very seldom feuds with seven or eight other people, though, so in a large family there is always someone left to turn to for consolation and love."

The point that siblings *know* each other so well was believed by many to be the key to the emotional security provided by a large family. According to Bossard and Boll, some informants felt that their own siblings had a better understanding of the problems that younger children faced than did their parents. They not only realized when and why their young siblings felt insecure, but also helped them through such difficult situations.

My oldest brother took my youngest brother to his first Scout meeting. I took him to his first day at school. When a child is faced with a new experience it must be a great comfort to know that someone is there who has been through it all before.

Mother spanked my third brother. Sister cried as hard as if she had been spanked and as soon as Mother left the room, she ran to his side, put her arm around him, and said through her tears, "You'll be all right, don't cry."

Three of us had mumps at the same time. We could console one another as we lay sick in bed.

The boys down the street and my second brother would get into a fight. The minute my eldest brother and I discovered it we were also in it, beating the other kid up or helping our little brother to hold his own. Surely it is a good feeling for a child to know there are others to help fight his battles, whether he be right or wrong.

For some children in the study, the security of the relationship with the brothers and sisters was closely related to the problem that the children all faced together. Often the children helped each other through the difficulties of coping with an inadequate mother or father, or difficult social circumstances. And some siblings felt that their security together came from the very fact that there was no opportunity for emotional "coddling" of any of them by the parents, with the exception perhaps of the youngest.

The picture of a childhood spent with several brothers and sisters as one of security, strength, and a rich shared world of play is of course only a partial one. Rivalry and competition were described too. Often the large families split into factions and cliques, or shifting alliances against particular children or subgroups of children. But they stressed rivalry less than did individuals from smaller families. It could well be that this was because these informants were recalling their childhood experiences, and tended to remember the better moments rather than the irritations of living with so many siblings. The children who were interviewed while still living at home did in fact stress conflict and rivalry more than the other informants.

In this chapter we have looked at the issue of why children differ so dramatically in the affection and hostility that they show toward their siblings, and specifically at the question of how the age gap, birth order, and gender of the siblings contribute to these differences. It is clear that if we want to explain the individual differences in how well brothers and sisters get along, and the ways in which they influence one another, we must move away from asking simply: Is it the age gap that matters? Is it the sex of the siblings that is crucial? We must realize first what a complicated equation we are dealing with when we ask what influences the relationship between the children in a family. Not only age and sex, but the personalities of the children, the size of the family, the social circumstances, and especially the children's relations with their parents must be taken into account. A great many factors affect the relationship between siblings. It is hardly surprising that we do not find simple clear connections between a child's position in the family, the sex of his siblings, and the way children get along or the way in which their personalities develop.

However, the studies of birth order and gender do help answer the questions raised by the book's first theme, which concerns the ways in which siblings influence one another's development. The sex and personality of the firstborn are, for instance, more likely to influence the laterborn children in a direct way than vice versa. How a first child feels about his or her sibling appears to influence the way in which their relationship develops from the earliest weeks. Firstborns are more likely to express ambivalence or hostility than laterborns. But the extent of intimacy and affection that a child feels and shows toward a sibling—which is probably of prime importance in *how* he or she influences the sibling—is not simply related to birth order, age gap, or gender.

We still know very little about the way in which the personalities of the individual children affect the quality of the relationship or vice versa. But it is clear that each child's relationship with the parents is closely implicated in many of the differences between siblings. It is to the connections between parent and sibling behavior that we turn next.

6 / Parents and Siblings

In every family there is a complex network of influences among the different family members. Parents treat their various children differently, and they respond to the differences in their children's personalities. The children exploit and enjoy different aspects of their family world. They watch—often jealously—their siblings and parents together, and react promptly to suspected favoritism. In this chapter we will look at these patterns of influence within the family. What kinds of differences are there in the way that parents treat their different children? Do these affect the children's relationships with each other?

Parents are often quite explicit about the different qualities that they enjoy in their different children, and about the different responses which the children draw from them. Here is a Cambridge mother talking about her children, aged nine, seven, and three: "I enjoy *different* things about each of the three. Sally's very up and down but when she's up she's marvellous and we have such laughs. I feel like I'm her age! Then Peter, he's such a calm and placid boy, it's a pleasure to talk with him and I love it that he somehow always, well not always but really *most* of the time, seems happy and easy and content, and *interested* in things. Eddie is much more anxious. I do worry about him more than the others, and I *fuss* over him I'm sure; my heart turns over sometimes when he looks alarmed or upset. I'm a different kind of person with him, somehow." With a large family, a mother has very different needs to serve among her different children. As a mother of six commented in Bossard and Boll's study: "Every time I walk through the house I have to be six different kinds of a mother. My 16-year-old boy needs one kind, my 15-year-old girl another, my 13-year-old boy another, and so on down to the baby. Then, at night, when my husband comes home, I must be a supervisor to see that all is quiet and peaceful in the household. Each of these seven needs me, and each for different reasons."

FIRSTBORNS AND LATERBORNS

It is widely held that parents are more easygoing and relaxed with their laterborn children, and that firstborns are more difficult to cope with. The Newsons' study suggested that the chief change in parents' behavior with a firstborn and a laterborn was a change from rigidity to flexibility, rather than from strictness to leniency. The mothers became more confident that the details of upbringing didn't matter too much—that they could depart from approved practice without disaster. Here is a quotation from a mother of three:

I think the main thing is that you acquire a sense of proportion, you see things in their proper perspective. For instance—Becky, as I said, still gets rocked to sleep on my lap every night of her life. Now I like that, and she likes it—partly, I suppose, because I expect her to be my last, but also because she's a nice cuddly dumpling and she likes the songs I sing to her then, and I like singing them. But now suppose it had been Ben, my eldest—and with Ben there was something similar, the bedtime bottle in his case—my mother or someone would have said to me, "But when is it going to *end?*"—and then I would have tried in a half-hearted sort of way to stop it, and we should all have been upset. But now I can see it in the perspective of growing up, and I know perfectly well, from experience of three children, that eventually she won't *want* to be rocked to sleep, because she'll prefer to have a little bedtime play in her nursery, or to read in bed for a while. There's a *natural progression* of things, which with your first child you're just not really aware of, and that's where most of the worry comes from, in my experience.

The results of the Nottingham study showed that laterborns were allowed more indulgent bedtimes, and that habits such as thumbsucking or holding comfort objects (dummies, "special" cloths, or toys) were more common among laterborn or only children. Such habits flourish in a more permissive atmosphere where time, patience, and indulgence are freely granted. Pressure on laterborn children over food fads and toilet training was frequently less severe than on the firstborn.

Children themselves are well aware of the differences in the degrees of indulgence their parents show. Here are two quotes from secondborn five-year-olds in Helen Koch's study: "I can hit him but he can't hit me." "Sometimes I take things from my brother. Mother says he's to give it to me."

It is easy to see that greater indulgence and protection of a younger child may exacerbate feelings of jealousy on the older child's part. Certainly the interview studies with children aged five, six, and seven show how vividly firstborns feel these disparities. The firstborn five- and six-year-olds in Koch's study were much more likely to feel that their mother favored the laterborn. The next quote, from the Cambridge studies, shows how the mother's role as mediator in the children's quarrels is seen by the firstborn. The interviewer has asked six-year-old Sally who usually wins the arguments and fights she has with her younger sister, Anny:

> *Sally:* Well, Anny is usually winning the arguments because she is the smallest.
> *Interviewer:* How does she do that? How does she win?
> *Sally:* Well, because Mummy tells me to do it because Anny is smaller than me. 'Cause if I was smaller than Anny I would have been winning the arguments. Mummy tells me to do it . . . Mummy tells me to do it and I can't say no to Mummy 'cause I'll get . . . That's why I've always got to do it. I never say, "No Mummy."
> *Interviewer:* So that's how Anny wins?
> *Sally:* Yeah.

There is no doubt that when children are young, mothers tend to champion the younger sibling. In quarrels between eighteen-month-olds or two-year-olds and their older siblings, mothers are three times more likely to prohibit or scold their firstborn child than their second-born—and it is certainly not the case that the firstborns are three times more likely than the babies to be the cause of the quarrel.

Many seven- and eight-year-olds continue to mind about the attention that their younger siblings receive, even though their parents go to great lengths to try to even the balance.

Are mothers in fact warmer and more nurturant as well as more protective toward their laterborn children than they were to their oldest, or are they simply more relaxed? Some studies report that mothers are indeed warmer and more attentive to their laterborn children. Others tell a different story. Those comparing the amount of time that mothers spend interacting with their first and laterborn children report that the laterborns get less attention from the parents. It is assumed that these differences in attention from the parents in the early years contribute to the differences between firstborns and laterborns in the ages at which they learn to talk, and their success on some tests of intelligence. What could explain the differences in the results of the studies? It is important to note that some studies compare the parents' behavior when *both* children are present, and it is in this situation that the firstborns often get lesser amounts of affectionate attention than the second- or laterborns. In contrast, the studies in which mothers are observed alone with either firstborn or laterborn children report that the first child tends to get more attention than the laterborn. Also important is the fact that for many firstborns there is a dramatic drop in parental attention with the birth of the second child. In the Cambridge study which followed families from before the birth of a second child through his or her infancy, although this major drop in attention did not last for many months after the infant's birth, the level of attention that the firstborns received from their mothers never again equalled what it had been before the second child arrived. In terms of their mothers' attention, the world was never again the same for the firstborn children, after the birth of their sibling.

There is yet another point. Not only are there differences in indulgence and maternal support for the different children within the family, but the pressure on a firstborn to "grow up" and be independent *because* there is a new baby is often quite explicit from the earliest weeks after the sibling's birth—a pressure acknowledged and often regretted by the mother, who is struggling to cope with more than one child. Many mothers in the Cambridge study commented that they now expected the firstborn to "play on his own" much more than formerly.

While firstborn children generally get more attention than laterborns, there remain important consistencies in mothers' behavior with their first- and laterborn children. For instance, compared with mothers generally, the mothers who play a lot with their first child also tend to play a lot with their second. And mothers who talk a lot to their first child also talk a lot to their second. Important features of a mother's "style" of interacting with her children carry over from one child to the next.

SAME-SEX AND DIFFERENT-SEX SIBLINGS

Differences in mothers' treatment of their children are linked to differences in how well same-sex siblings and different-sex siblings relate to each other. Studies of young siblings have found that mothers show more intense and playful attention to their second child if he or she differs in sex from the first. It could be that this *contributes* to the hostility shown by young siblings who differ in sex: the firstborn reacts to the warmth the mother shows the second by directing hostility at the baby. Or it could be that the mothers are *responding* to the hostility they see between the children, and are trying to "make up" to the baby for the lack of affection from the older sibling. Or both of these effects could be important. A study conducted in Canada with slightly older children did not find that mothers were more affectionate or attentive to their secondborn if the child differed in sex from the firstborn; but the mothers *were* more consistent in their treatment of the two children if they were the same sex. Rona Abramovitch and her colleagues argue plausibly that this differential treatment of siblings in different-sex pairs may well contribute to the greater hostility and jealousy between them.

Support for this argument comes from a California study in which six- and seven-year-old girls, their older sisters, and their mothers played a series of games together. Brenda Bryant and Susan Crockenberg found that the behavior of the two children toward each other depended in part on how each child was treated by the mother *relative to the other child*. In families in which one child was helped and comforted by her mother and the other child was not, both children were notably unhelpful and unsupportive toward each other. Additional support for the idea comes from Helen Koch's interviews with five- and six-year-olds: secondborn children with a different-sex older sibling referred more often to differential treatment by the parents than did secondborn siblings in same-sex pairs.

Differences in mothers' behavior toward their various children depend partly on the sex of the older child. Victor Cicirelli, in his "teaching" experiments, found that mothers gave more explanation and feedback to children with older brothers than to those with older sisters. He suggested that this was because mothers implicitly or explicitly relinquish some of their caregiving functions to older sisters, whereas they do not do this with older sons. There may be a link between the degree to which a mother ignores her younger child and the amount of support and assistance which the older child offers the younger. In the California study, the older sisters were more supportive of the younger in those families in which the mother ignored the younger's requests for help. The results suggest that in this situation at least older sisters "step in," to support and care for younger sisters who they feel are being ignored.

INFLUENCE BETWEEN MOTHER AND SIBLINGS

The way in which a mother behaves toward one child in her family is intimately related to the way in which the other children behave toward her and toward each other. And the more closely one examines the connections between family relationships, the more complex the patterns appear to be. For instance, in the Cambridge study of firstborn children before and after the sibling birth, the results showed that in families with a particularly playful and intense relationship between firstborn girls and their mothers before and immediately following the birth of a second child, the girl was relatively hostile to the baby. And after one year the secondborn was particularly hostile to the older sister. This pattern was not explained by the mother's behavior toward her second child: even when the extent of the mother's playful attention to the secondborn was taken into account, there was still a link between the extent to which the mother had played with the firstborn and the hostile behavior of the two children toward each other. But the relationship between mother and second child was important, too. To make the pattern even more complicated (and even more convincing in commonsense terms), the results also showed that in families in which the mothers were particularly affectionate and friendly with their secondborn babies at the eight-month stage, the two children were especially hostile to each other six months later.

The mother's behavior with her firstborn had another influence on the relationship that developed between the siblings. There were marked differences between the mothers in the way in which they talked to the firstborn about the baby's needs, feelings, and wants in the early weeks. In some families the mother discussed the baby with the first child, almost as an equal. She commented on what the baby might be feeling or needing, drawing the firstborn's attention to the baby's interest in the older sibling, to what the baby appeared to enjoy , and to the baby's state. Some examples: "She likes looking at you." "Is she cross at being woken up?" "I think he's watching you. Can you see him looking? I think he's watching you." "He likes you to kiss his face like that." "He won't smile when you're yelling 'cause it makes him a bit upset." "He's looking at something there—my dressing gown—he likes the color." "Listen to little Jamie; he wants his bottle." These mothers often asked the first children, even those who were barely two years old, what they thought should be done with the baby. They discussed *why* the baby should be crying or happy. They drew the first child into caring for the new (and often difficult) family member.

Tim W. and Mother
Mother: Tim, do you reckon he's hungry? Or is he just waiting for his bath? . . . Shall we roll him over and see if he likes going on his tummy? . . . Oh, what shall we do with him? I think we'd better hurry up and bathe him anyway. Let's give him a bath. Can you help me with the bath water?
Tim to Baby: Baby! Baby!
Mother: That's right. You talk to him and cheer him up.

Penny D. and Mother:
Penny: Got make his wind [he has to burp].
Mother: Got make his wind?
Penny: Yeah.
Mother to Baby: Come on, Harry!
Penny: [laughs]
Mother: Are you going to come and help me? I'm not
    doing very well, am I?
Penny: [pats baby; baby gives slight grunt] Ooh!
Mother: That was just a grunt.
Penny to Baby: Hello, Harry! Hello, Harry! [baby looks
    at her; child turns to observer in triumph]
Penny to Observer: Look!
Mother: He gave us a smile yesterday, didn't he?
Penny to Baby: Give me a smile.
Mother to Baby: Give us a smile.
Penny to Baby: Whee! [kisses baby]
Mother: He'll eat your nose if you're not careful, won't
    he?
Penny: He eat nose.
Mother: Is he eating your nose? Or giving you a kiss?
Penny: Giving a kiss.

The mothers and firstborns in these families often
delighted together in the baby's achievements and behavior. Their shared pleasure and amusement was evident in their discussion of the baby.

Ian W. and Mother
Ian to Baby: [showing bear to baby; Mother is at the other
    end of room, washing clothes] Look baby, look! [Baby
    looks]
Ian to Mother: Look Mummy, look!
Mother: What is he doing, Ian? Mmm? What is he doing?
Ian: Look. He's looking. Look. He's looking.
Mother: He likes pretty colors, doesn't he? Not near his

face. Look, he likes these, doesn't he? No, he's only interested in his food at the moment. We'll have to put that in his cot. Then he can see it, eh?

Most strikingly, in the families in which these discussions about the baby were common in the early weeks, the firstborns continued through the next year to be particularly friendly to their sibling, and by fourteen months the secondborns were especially friendly to the older child. Even as young as two years, children are interested in and reflect upon the feelings and wishes of their siblings, and mothers who encourage this concern are fostering a loving relationship between the children that will continue for years.

FATHERS

What about fathers? Research until now has focused chiefly upon mothers and their children. But of course children's relationships with their fathers are enormously important, and when we bring the father into the picture the patterns of mutual influence become even more complicated.

Many firstborns are particularly jealous when their father plays with the younger child. One firstborn in the Cambridge studies put it firmly to her mother: "Daddy is *not* Ronnie's daddy." And another mother described a typical reaction on the part of her daughter: "She minds him [father] holding him much more than when I do. I think she takes me and him [baby] for granted. But she looks at her dad in a special way when he's with the baby." In many families in which the first child had a particularly intense relationship with the father, the siblings got along less well during the next year—paralleling the pattern in families in which the firstborn daughter was very closely involved with the mother before the sibling's birth. But the picture was by no means a bleak one; in families in which the firstborn was closely involved with the father before the sibling's birth, the escalation of difficulties and conflict with the *mother* after the sibling's birth was less marked. The father's relationship with the firstborn can, it seems, "buffer" the firstborn against some of the trauma of being "displaced" in the affections of the mother. For many children the relationship with the father becomes increasingly close and intense during the year following the sibling's birth. Of course, this may in part be because the fathers become more interested in their children as they grow up from babies to children. Three quotes from the Cambridge studies illustrate this increasing interest, which more than 40 percent of the fathers showed as their children grew up:

> He prefers older children. He's more of a *child-lover* than a *baby-lover*.

> He isn't really interested in babies; more interested as they grow up.

> There's definitely a difference now. He enjoys her coming with him fishing or to the garage. He *makes* more time to be with her now.

As the children grow up, it is quite common for one child to develop a particularly close relationship with the father, while the others may be closer to the mother. Frequently mothers will comment that "she's a 'daddy's girl,' while this one is all for me!" This is just one example of how children exploit and experience very different lives within the same family world, and one way in which differences between siblings could arise.

If you watch the way in which one child responds when her mother or father engages in games or play with her brother or sister, you can see just how important the relationship between the parent and the other sibling is for most young children. The reaction is often immediate: it may be an enthusiastic attempt to join the parent and sibling, or a more ambivalent action that has the effect of disrupting their play, or an immediate demand for attention. It is rare for a young child to ignore what is happening between the sibling and mother or father. It is not just the older child who monitors and responds quickly to play between parent and sibling: by the end of the first year, many laterborn children are violently and effectively assertive in pushing between mother and older child. And many mothers comment that by the second year it is the second child who is the most jealous.

But children differ very much in their responses to the games between sibling and parent. When the siblings are very young, children with same-sex siblings are likely to join mother and sibling in a friendly way, as are children who reacted to the birth of the sibling with positive interest. In contrast, children who have reacted to the birth by becoming particularly naughty and demanding, or who are in temperament rather difficult and irritable, are more likely to protest at their mothers' games with the sibling, and less likely to ignore these games by continuing with their own pursuits. Here are some examples from the Cambridge studies:

Joanne R. (firstborn) and Donna
Mother to Donna: You play with that one.
Joanne: It's mine! It's mine!
Mother to Donna: Well, have a look at the book then.
   Where's the book?

Joanne: It's mine!
Mother to Donna: [looking at book] Pretty!
Joanne: Donna will tear it.

Fay G. (firstborn) and Ruby
Mother to Ruby: [commenting on her playing] Are you
  enjoying yourself, Ruby?
Fay: She can't have that any more.

Virginia L. (firstborn) and Malcolm
Mother to Malcolm: [playing with Lego] I'll make you a
  little car, Malcolm.
Virginia: Well, I want one.
Mother to Malcolm: Shall I make you a car? Mmm?
Virginia: Don't let him have the red pieces.
Mother to Malcolm: [picking him up and imitating his
  noises]Wawwaw! Wawwaw!
Virginia: Can I sit beside you? Can I sit on knee?
Mother to Virginia: Is that just because Malcolm's up here?
Virginia: Yes.
Mother: Come on then.

PATTERNS OVER TIME: BOYS AND GIRLS

In families in which the parents had a particularly
intense and close relationship with a firstborn daughter,
the girls were likely to behave in unfriendly and hostile
ways to the baby sibling as he or she grew up (especially
if the secondborn was a "he"). By the time the secondborn was a year old, he was likely in turn to be hostile
to his sister, from whom he had received punishment
and aggression rather than warmth. It is easy to see this
pattern as a natural response on the part of the elder
child to the displacement she has experienced. But there
is another way to see this link. We can focus on the
other side of the coin, and recognize that in families in
which the firstborn girl had a relatively detached rela-

tionship with her mother the sibling relationship often developed as an especially warm and affectionate one—a relationship of real emotional significance to the older child. One vivid illustration of this from the Cambridge study of the sibling birth was the finding that in families in which the mother was depressed after the sibling's birth, and emotionally detached from the firstborn, the siblings frequently developed a very close and friendly attachment.

The differences in the responses of boys and girls in this study are intriguing. Why should it be the girls who showed this pattern, and not the boys? The pattern could, of course, be an artifact of the relatively small sample. The results must be confirmed for a different sample before one generalizes in too cavalier a fashion from this particular study. But there are some grounds for thinking that *displacement* by a sibling, and the shattering decrease in maternal attention which accompanies it, have different meanings for girls and for boys. There is some evidence that there is a clearer pattern of association between mothers' behavior toward their daughters, and the girls' behavior and personality later on, than there is between mothers' behavior toward their sons, and the boys' development. It is possible, then, that boys are in some ways more independent of their mothers' influence than are girls. Nancy Chodorow has argued that girls' developing sense of *who they are* and their self-esteem are closely bound up with identification with their mothers. In the case of boys, she suggests, this sense of self is bound up with a sense of *difference* from their mothers. If girls do indeed identify closely with their mothers, then it is easy to see why being displaced from a close and intense relationship with the mother should have an especially upsetting effect, particularly when this "dethronement" happens around the age of two or three years, when young children are just beginning to develop a sense of who they are.

If we are to understand why children differ so much in the extent of affection and hostility that they show toward their siblings, we must take account of the close links between the siblings' relationship and each child's relationship with the parents. The patterns are complicated: how a mother behaves with her firstborn daughter before a sibling is born is linked to the extent of affection and hostility between the children a year later; differences in maternal behavior toward one child relative to the other are also linked to differences in the siblings' behavior to each other. We don't know the direction of influence here. It seems plausible that the correlations may reflect causal influence in both directions—that parents affect the sibling relationship *and* that the siblings' relationship influences the parents' behavior toward each child. The parental relationship appears to be more closely linked to differences in the way in which children behave toward their siblings than are the old favorites, age gap and gender. Differences in parental behavior may indeed help explain those gender differences that have been found. For instance, parental behavior appears to be implicated in the greater hostility between different-sex siblings than between same-sex siblings during the preschool years.

For parents, these generalizations leave open an important question: What practical implications follow from these studies? It is difficult to draw any simple practical lessons from the particular patterns of parent-child and sibling-sibling relationships. But, clearly, it would be wrong to blame parents for the hostility between their children. No one could blame a mother for the intense relationship she has with her firstborn daughter (though psychiatrists do believe that an overprotective relationship between parent and firstborn is likely to lead to an extremely hostile sibling relationship). The area in which parents are seen as particularly responsible for the quality of the relationship between the siblings is that of quarreling and aggression. Here the parent manuals are quite outspoken about the importance of parental influence. Is this a reasonable view to take? Let us look at some of the problems that parents face in coping with young siblings, including the issue of quarrels and aggression.

7 / Problems for Parents

There is no doubt that the arrival of a brother or sister is usually traumatic for a young firstborn child. People have commented on this for hundreds of years. Much of the early writing about this "dethronement" was based on retrospective case histories retracing the experiences of very troubled children. Because these accounts reconstruct the child's experiences, often long after the event, it is difficult to interpret the account of the child's behavior and to generalize from the findings to "normal" children. It is not at all clear what kinds of predictions can be made about the vulnerability of other children on the basis of these case histories.

However, there are now a number of studies that carefully trace the behavior of children before and after the birth of a sibling. They show how common are the different forms of disturbance after the arrival of a second child. They also give some idea of why particular children become troubled and others cope well, and which problems are likely to persist and which are most transient.

PROBLEMS FOLLOWING THE ARRIVAL OF A SIBLING

Most firstborn children show some signs of being upset in the weeks following a sibling's birth. Five separate interview studies report that the majority of children show disturbed behavior: the proportion of children with increased problems ranged from over 50 percent to 92 percent of the children studied. One of the difficulties with interpreting these interview studies is that the changes in the children's behavior were described from the *mothers' point of view*. In itself this is obviously important; but in order to assess the changes and to understand *why* the children changed we need, in addition, to have direct information about the changes in family life which accompanied the birth. In one of the Cambridge studies my colleagues and I observed the children *and* interviewed the mothers both before and in the months following the birth of the sibling, and the results gave all too clear a picture of the disturbance in the children's behavior. The most common change was an increase in naughtiness, shown by 93 percent of the children:

> *Mother of Sylvia S.:* She always was naughty, but now she won't do *anything* I ask. I send her up to bed and try not to smack [spank]. I don't really believe in it; anyway, it doesn't do any good. She's rude, cheeky, into things, defiant, disobedient.

> *Mother of Joanne R.:* She's got very selfish—wants everything she can see. Gets very cross if she's told to wait.

More than half the children also became more tearful and clingy, and several children became more withdrawn.

Mother of Jim E.: He cries at everything. I can't tell him off for anything.

Mother of Dianne H.: There's more tears over frustration. She's more sensitive to things. As though life's a bit hard all 'round—as if she's [got] more to cope with and she's not quite sure how to cope with it.

Mother of Arnold H.: It's not so bad now as it was at first, when he was naughty, crying, and difficult. He didn't do anything I asked. So bad-tempered. Anything you said no to, he cried. Now it seems as if he's in a wee world of his own. So quiet. I think he's feeling pushed out. If anyone comes, he used to get so excited. Now he's so quiet.

There were changes, too, in sleeping and toileting behavior. Toilet training, for instance, broke down in half of the children who were trained at the time of the birth. Aggression toward the baby was at this stage very rare. It was the mothers, rather than the siblings, who took the brunt of the firstborns' difficult behavior.

Different kinds of disturbed behavior after the birth of a sibling are not closely related. The children in Cambridge who developed sleeping problems were, for instance, not necessarily the children who had become more demanding or withdrawn. And, strikingly, the children who were most interested and affectionate toward the baby were sometimes those who were in other ways very disturbed after the birth. Children who developed sleeping problems or who were very naughty and demanding were in some cases also very affectionate toward the baby, interested in caring for him and in trying to entertain and comfort him. The same children who showed increased problem behavior also often showed an increase in independence and maturity following the birth. They insisted on feeding themselves, dressing themselves, or going to the toilet alone. These results show that the idea of a simple reaction of disturbance following the sibling's birth is misleading. Children react in different ways, and their reaction is frequently a combination of retrogression, anger, distress, and increasingly mature behavior. The three questions which most concern parents and clinicians are: How long do the different forms of disturbance persist? Which children are most vulnerable to the constellation of changes following the birth? How can they best be helped through this stressful period?

The answer to the first question is on the whole a very encouraging one. In the Cambridge study of the effects of the sibling birth, most of the behavior problems had largely disappeared by the time the baby was eight months old. Not only did most of the problems disappear, but there was no link between the incidence of problems and the development of a poor relationship between the siblings. The exception to this hopeful story was the incidence of fearful, worrying, and anxious behavior. Children of this age often have particular fears, and in some of the firstborn children these became so marked that they seriously interfered in the children's lives. One three-year-old was terrified of the vacuum cleaner, of the dark and of water in the bathtub. Another would not go into the garden if he heard a plane, and another would not go into the street if he saw a cat. Thirty-eight percent of the children in the study showed an increase in marked fears during the year following the sibling's birth. The children also tended to show an increase in ritualistic behaviors: "Bedtime, bathtime, and mealtime rituals were particularly strong, as were rituals for saying goodbye to parents. One child would not go to sleep unless all his teddies had been kissed, his mother had kissed him between each bar of the cot, and the door was left open at a specific angle. Another insisted at meals that her mother put her food in a certain dish, that each member of the family have a particular place- ment, and that her mother blow on her food three times. Thirty-five percent of the sample increased in ritualistic behavior of this kind, and only 8 percent decreased." Several of the children became more worried about things being lost, changed, or broken; about "dangers"; or about particular television programs. Said the mother of one young boy: "He's very concerned about losing things, and about my hurting myself. Or about dangers. He 'reports' to his dad about me, or to me about his dad, if we've done dangerous things—'naughty things,' he calls it." Since large-scale studies following children over time suggest that fearful, worrying behavior in three- and four-year-olds persists over several years and is linked to difficult behavior in eight-year-olds, the increase in such anxious behavior after the sibling's birth is a cause for some concern. It was also found that in families in which the children reacted to the sibling's birth by *with- drawing*, the relationship that developed between the siblings over the next years was likely to be hostile and full of conflict.

On the question of *which* children were most vulner- able, the results provided some surprises. The extreme forms of reaction were not linked in any simple way to the ages of the firstborns at the birth, or to their sex (though boys were more likely to become withdrawn), or to whether the child had been separated from the mother at the time of the birth by her going to the hos- pital. Children under five years old are more likely to be upset by the sibling's birth than children over five. Below five years, however, the age of the child at the time of the birth seems to be much less important than the child's particular personality. Children who tend to be irritable or moody, difficult to manage, and emotional about changes or frustration respond with most disturbance to the birth of a sibling.

The second feature that stood out as important was the child's relationship with his or her parents before the birth of the sibling. In families in which there had been a high level of confrontation between mother and firstborn before the birth of the sibling, the firstborns were reported to behave in a particularly irritating and intrusive way with the new baby. On the other hand, in families in which the child had had a particularly close relationship with the father before the birth, the escalation of conflict with the mother after the birth was much less marked than in families in which the child was less intensely involved with the father.

The third aspect of the events surrounding the birth that was linked to the children's reaction was the mother's state of tiredness or depression following the baby's birth. In families in which the mother was extremely tired or depressed after the birth, the firstborns were more likely to become withdrawn. The association between the mother's depressed mood and the child's withdrawal is not a surprising one, but the direction of the causal link is unknown. It could be that the withdrawal of the first child increases the mother's depression, though it seems more likely that the child's behavior is a response to the mother's state.

Does preparing the child by explaining what is in store help? There is no evidence that preparation decreases the probability of a disturbed or jealous reaction. This may be because it is difficult to measure the differences in the extent of preparation that children have been given. Most mothers talk to their first children about the impending arrival, and most firstborns have had some contact with babies. But the real problem in com-

paring different degrees of preparation is that the meaning of the explanation will be very different for, say, an
eighteen-month-old and a five-year-old. And however
well prepared a child is, however clearly he seems to
understand what the sibling's birth will entail, he may
be overwhelmed by his emotional reaction to the real
event.

There is little evidence that if children visit their mothers in the hospital, a disturbed reaction to the birth will
be less likely. In fact, there is little connection between
children's first reactions to the baby—their responses to
being "introduced"—and their behavior over the next
few weeks.

The Cambridge studies did give some clear hints as
to what particular aspects of the events surrounding the
birth upset the children most. First, it was during the
time that the mother was occupied with the baby—
bathing, caring for, cuddling, or feeding the baby—that
naughty behavior by the firstborn greatly increased. It
was not breastfeeding per se that was particularly upsetting. Indeed, the escalation of conflict which was noted
during bottle feeding was not apparent during breastfeeding. This is probably partly because mothers who
are about to breastfeed make more elaborate prepara-
tions for the demands and requests of the first child
before they begin to feed the baby. In the Cambridge
study of the effects of the sibling birth, the breastfeeding
mothers collected drinks, potty, books, crayons, or puz-
zles *before* the feeding began, so that when the inevitable
demands for attention came from the firstborns, they
were well prepared with distractions. It was clear from
these observations that breastfeeding was not a situation
of particular trauma for the first children. Here the opinions and advice of the parent manuals are misleading.
Benjamin Spock, for instance, advises mothers that it is

better "as far as is convenient to take care of her [the new baby] while the older one is not around," and comments that "many young children feel the greatest jealousy when they see their mother feeding the baby, especially at the breast." The Cambridge study shows, in contrast, that a mother's decision to breastfeed her second baby will not necessarily subject her firstborn child to extra stress. The practical lesson is clear: if parents are prepared for demands and requests for attention when they are caring for the new baby, the likelihood of conflict will decrease.

A second practical lesson concerns the amount of attention that the first child receives, and the changes in his or her routine after the sibling's birth. For the majority of children in the Cambridge study, the arrival of the baby caused a dramatic decrease in the playful attention that the mother paid to the firstborn, and also major changes in the day-to-day life of the firstborn. Many mothers felt that these changes in routine contributed greatly to the disturbed behavior of their firstborn.

> Even when there was no separation from the mother, the events surrounding the birth were enough to distort the relationship and destroy its harmony. And to the mothers, a prime contribution to the child's difficult behaviour was the change in his expected routine. The grandparents and fathers who acted as surrogate mothers were described as simply *not knowing* how important the small details of the child's expected routine were to his well-being. A constantly recurring theme was that not only did the substitute mother frequently forget that the child needed his special cup, or his particular bedtime routine, or ritual game, but "she" also disrupted his expectation or understanding of what was *allowed*— either by overindulgence or by overrestriction.

Mother of Harvey M.: I think he's a bit more defiant. Sometimes he *grins* when I tell him off. He thinks he can get away with it. So he's had a few smacks lately, but I put this down to my parents' being here last week. My dad took him out to the shops every day—spoiling him, in other words.

Mother of Laura W.: While I was away she was taken out a good deal—a big social whirl. Now she's *got* to get used to having less of that. But my mum wasn't very indulgent with her; in fact, she got fed up with her. That didn't help.

Mother of Tim W.: His routine is all messed up. He's upset by the constant visitors.

These comments bring home to us the importance that the child attaches to his or her expected daily routine, to a world in which things happen with comfortable predictability. And they show, too, how crucial the mother is as the architect of that world, a world that is both intelligible and dependable for the child, and how easily the coordination of mother and child can be disrupted.

It seems especially important to try to minimize the drop in attention which the first child receives after the birth. As already noted, talking to the first child about the baby as a person, and encouraging the firstborn to help and become involved with the baby, seem to help to ease the stress and to foster a good relationship between the children. The other practical findings from the Cambridge study are really common sense. Mothers need all the help that they can get during the early weeks. They are likely to have a very demanding and difficult firstborn to cope with, as well as a newborn baby and a long series of broken nights. Over half the mothers in our study were getting less than five hours sleep per twenty-four hours at three weeks after the birth. Several became exhausted and strained, and their relationship with the firstborn clearly suffered very much. These comments were made by two mothers three weeks after the birth of their second child:

> *Mother of Laura W.:* I'm very low. I feel like murdering her. I dread the sound of her feet along the corridor. I've wept for two weeks.

> *Mother of Sylvie S.:* I'm not quite as exhausted as last week—still, very tired. Very edgy and irritable. I've got so I can't stand her. She has me in tears every day. It's bad really.

This degree of exhaustion and irritability with the first child was, fortunately, relatively uncommon. And it is encouraging to know that most of the behavior problems that these toddlers showed after the birth improved greatly after the first few months, and that the children who were particularly difficult and demanding were not especially likely to get on badly with their siblings over the years that followed.

QUARRELS AND FIGHTS

"It's the fighting that gets me down," says the mother of Charlie (three) and Robbie (six). "They just know how to needle each other, and it's bicker, bicker, bicker. Then one of them lashes out, and they're really at each other. It's worse when Robbie gets home from school—I suppose they're both tired—but every day we have the same kind of scene. It drives me wild, really." Most brothers and sisters argue a good deal, and many quarrel and fight uninhibitedly, whether they are not yet in school or well into middle childhood. For many parents these arguments and the escalation into physical fights are a matter of concern and worry.

By middle childhood, physical fights are far more common between siblings than between children outside the family. Among the seven-year-olds in the Newsons' Nottingham study, only 7 percent fought *often* with other children, but 29 percent fought *often* with siblings. Sixty-four percent of the children were said to fight either sometimes or often with their brothers or sisters, and only 32 percent with other children. There is an interesting difference between boys and girls here: twice as many boys were involved in fights outside the family, but within a family girls were just as likely as boys to come to blows. The Newsons' point out that since this frequent fighting by both boys and girls is hidden from outsiders, parents are unaware of how common it is. Since it seems that their *own* children fight a great deal more than the children in other families, many parents feel concerned, and indeed inadequate in their handling of fights. But the crucial point is that while the fighting that they witness in their own home *is* worse and more frequent than anything they see in the streets and playgrounds, or in other people's homes, it is almost certainly *not* worse than the fighting that takes place in the privacy of family life in these other homes.

There are startling differences between families in the violence and frequency of the conflict, as the children's comments in Helen Koch's study show. Compare the quotation at the beginning of this section with the comments of the mother of Duncan (three) and Robin (fourteen months): "They rarely fight. If Robin has something, Duncan may take it, but he always gives him something else. Duncan's always been interested in him—fetched and carried for him. Now it's on the other foot—Robin gets things for *him*. Duncan always holds his hand, walks him up the road. The last month or so they've really played; the latest thing is these chasing games—quite complicated ones. And they do comfort each other." How can these differences between families be explained? Advice books for parents often lay the blame for frequent quarrels on the parents: "When the baby is mobile," write the Calladines, "this is when sibling quarrels usually get under way . . . How the parent handles all this determines whether or not this becomes a reactive rivalrous situation." How well is this view supported by the studies of siblings? How do parents handle sibling quarrels, and to what do they attribute the conflict?

Parents take very different views about the extent to which they should intervene in children's quarrels, or whether the children should be left to sort it out for themselves. Some parents stress that the children are going to have to cope with fights and hostility outside the home, and thus must learn *at home* to be independent. Other parents feel that they should act as arbitrators, and try to get each child to understand the other's point of view—especially if the children have resorted to physical violence. There is a trend in Britain for middle-class mothers to take an involved part as mediators in quarrels, whereas working-class mothers are more likely to emphasize the importance of children's learning "to stand on their own two feet." But within different social-class groups, opinions on arbitration still vary enormously. A mother's attitude toward her children's behavior in quarrels within the family is inevitably colored by what experiences the siblings are likely to have with children outside the family.

Some common themes emerge from studies of parents' responses to quarrels. Weapons are generally frowned upon ("They can't do much damage with their fists . . . but when it comes to sticks or spades . . . ").

Hitting is usually described as permissible only in retaliation. Biting is considered a particularly serious of-
fense; in both the Cambridge and Nottingham studies,
retaliation to biting was often encouraged. Sometimes
the mother herself bit the child who was the biter—"to
show what it feels like."

As we have seen, firstborns often feel that their parents favor and support the laterborns in any dispute. In
fact, many mothers comment that they usually assume
a dispute to be the firstborn's fault, especially while the
other children are very young, and then catch themselves blaming the older child unfairly.

What about the question of parental responsibility for
frequent quarrels within the family? Two general points
must be made before we consider the research findings
and views of "experts." First, it is often the case that
one child in the family is mainly responsible for the
fights, or that one pair of siblings within a large family
don't get along. Here are one mother from Nottingham
(from the Newsons' study) and one from Cambridge
describing the fights within their respective families:

> *Truckdriver's wife:* She plays with Brendan [aged two and
> a half] *all* the time. They're very good friends, and
> they *don't* quarrel. She will share, there's nothing sel-
> fish about her in that respect, at least where Brendan's
> concerned. Now Derek, he's the next one up [five],
> and her, they fight like blacks, they can *never* agree
> over *anything*. June always wants Derek's chair and
> Derek always wants June's spoon. I've got a set of
> cutlery and they've all got different-coloured handles,
> and of course each of them has got their own colour,
> knife, fork, and spoon, you see. Well, as soon as Derek
> comes in he'll make a dive for June's colour, and then
> she'll want his chair, and so it goes on, you see. Yes,
> they're the two that fight.

Mother of Dickie (six), Erin (three), and Carol (fourteen months):
  Well, Dickie and Erin they just argue all the time. Fight
  over the slightest thing. Yet they're both so sweet with
  Carol—they'd do anything for her.

Clearly in these cases it can't be any *general* features of
the parents' child-rearing practices that are chiefly responsible for the quarrels, because the other children
within the family get along well. Siblings don't choose
to spend their early lives together—they are forced to
live together. We shouldn't be surprised if in some cases
they find it very difficult to get along, and parents certainly shouldn't blame themselves for the fact that two
individuals continually rub each other the wrong way.

Second, the very fact that quarrels are so common in
families with young children is, in its way, reassuring.
Parents shouldn't feel that they have failed in some special way if there is a lot of conflict between their children,
since the majority of children quarrel a lot in the early
years.

There have been relatively few studies of the consequences of different parental strategies for dealing with
sibling quarrels. One view of such quarrels is that children are aggressive toward their siblings primarily in
order to get the attention of their parents. According to
this view, when parents intervene in sibling quarrels
they are doing their children a "disservice," by providing them with "inappropriate" attention and by depriv-
ing them of the opportunity to learn how to resolve their
own disputes. One study of twelve families examined
the effectiveness of "nonintervention" by teaching parents to stay out of sibling fights: the families kept diaries
of sibling conflict, and a follow-up study of the families
eight months after the "parent training" suggested that
the frequency of quarrels had decreased. A second study
suggested that a daily "special time" set aside for play-

ing with a difficult child was also effective in reducing sibling conflict. A third study tried a combination of strategies: parents were encouraged not to intervene in quarrels, and children were rewarded for avoiding conflict and for cooperative play. Both types of strategy in the third study were equally effective and the level of conflict continued to decrease, according to a follow-up one month later.

Can we derive simple "rules of thumb" for parents from these studies? There are three problems with using this research to draw general conclusions about the handling of sibling conflict. First, the studies are based on the assumption that all sibling quarrels are essentially bids for parental attention. This view reflects the notion that the central core of the relationship between the siblings is one of rivalry—a notion that, as we have seen, gives a very partial and misleading picture of the sibling relationship. Interestingly, Benjamin Spock's *Baby and Child Care* gives advice that is based on this view: "To a greater or lesser degree, children quarrel because of their jealousy, because each would like to be favored by the parents. When a parent is always ready to take sides, in the sense of trying to decide who is right and who is wrong, it encourages them to quarrel soon again. Each hopes each time to win the parents' favor and see the other scolded."

The second problem with this noninterventionist advice is that there are many parents who simply cannot stand back and let their children hurt each other—even verbally. Such behavior offends and upsets them deeply. Recall the quotation from *Anna Karenina*, describing Darya Alexandrovna's feeling that "darkness had swooped down on her life" when she found Tanya and Grisha fighting so violently. We should surely respect these parents' values, and not assume that such parents should be "trained" out of such a response.

The third problem is that the studies are, in scientific terms, very limited in scope and certainly need replication, before we can have much confidence that we have uncovered the processes through which such interventions are effective, if indeed they are.

But there *are* some practical lessons to be drawn from the more general research on aggression and altruism in children. A firm and reasonably consistent response to children's physical aggression or unkindness *in the context of a loving and warm relationship* between parents and child seems to work most effectively in encouraging children's altruism and sensitivity to others. One recent study of very young children showed particularly clearly that a child's concern for others was most effectively fostered in families in which the mother drew the child's attention clearly and forcefully to the consequences of his unkindness and aggression for the other person, and firmly prohibited such actions, but in which the mother was also warm and loving to the child. There's a parallel here perhaps with the finding that in families in which the mother talked to the firstborn about the baby as a person with feelings and desires and needs, the children were likely to develop an affectionate and friendly relationship.

Another general lesson from the research on aggression is that frequent physical punishment seems to make children increasingly physically aggressive themselves.

There is also some evidence that if families are under stress—financial, emotional—then aggression and quarreling between the children are more common. It is not known precisely how this link arises, but it seems likely that stress and tension in parents' lives will make them more irritable and less relaxed with their children. Most parents know only too well how their own irritability influences their children's behavior toward them *and* toward each other. As one mother in the Cambridge studies put it: "They are difficult sometimes, yes— arguing and fighting and *mean* to each other. But I've noticed, you know, that it has quite a lot to do with *my* mood. If things are going well for me, I can laugh them out of it. But some days I just can't, and then it seems to go from bad to worse till we're all screaming at each other." The practical lesson here is an obvious one. Whatever makes a mother's life more tolerable and relaxed—help from husband or grandmother, work away from the house, a break from the children, help with marital problems—is likely to ease the tension between the children.

Parents' attitudes toward physical aggression in boys are often different from their attitudes toward aggression shown by girls. If researchers are to offer any useful advice to parents, there must be more careful studies which take account of different kinds of quarrels between siblings, different parental strategies, and differences in parents' feelings about aggressive behavior. Research of this sort has, in fact, been conducted with very aggressive children.

Extreme aggression between siblings—which is luckily rather rare—is much more difficult for parents to cope with than the relatively short-lived problems that follow the second sibling's birth. Gerry Patterson studied the behavior of very aggressive boys at home and at school, and found that siblings were involved in around 60 percent of the problem boys' "coercive" behavior. Siblings rather than parents appeared to be the family members who primarily elicited hitting and teasing from the aggressive children. During exchanges between these children, the younger siblings usually assumed the "victim" role and submitted to attacks by their older brothers. This submissive behavior, Patterson argues, causes the older brothers to increase the frequency of their attacks. Then the younger siblings begin to retaliate by being aggressive in turn, and this leads to further aggression. The siblings of these very aggressive boys are far more aggressive than the siblings of nonaggressive, "normal" children. Even when the researchers separated out the aggressive actions by the siblings that were committed *in response* to the problem children's aggressive overtures, the level of aggression shown by the siblings was very high, especially for boys.

The follow-up studies which Patterson conducted showed that the poor relationship between the siblings was linked to later delinquency. It is important to note, however, that the time spent with the sibling and the poor relationship with the sibling were both higher in families in which there was little organization, poor discipline by the parents, and little parental monitoring of the children. This link between continuing behavior problems in children, difficulties for the siblings of problem children, and disrupted or stressful family life is also relevant to families in which there is a mentally retarded or handicapped child. No simple connections should be inferred between a problem child's behavior and that of his "normal" sibling—it is *family* patterns that are at issue.

GROWING UP WITH A HANDICAPPED SIBLING

Here is seven-year-old Simon talking about his older brother David, aged nine, a Down's syndrome child:

> My brother is mentally handicapped. It is very difficult to speak to him. I find it rather easy to understand what he is saying. I think that is because I used to sleep in

ing with him on the sands. Each year they would say, "I wonder if Philip will go in this time; shall we try this with him; shall we try that with him?" We got him in last year and couldn't get him out.

The children in this family, and their friends, very much accept Philip as their responsibility.

Mrs. Mercer: He is the youngest of six children, which I think makes it a lot easier. I have got my others who are normal, bright kids who give me the satisfaction of their intellectual achievements, and this one is really like having a friendly dog around the place. We pat him on the head and spoil him . . . In fact he doesn't talk; but I suppose we don't really stimulate him enough at home, we give in to him too easily; but it has its advantages from my point of view, in that I am not so wrapped up in him.

Hannam: What about the rest of the family?

Mrs. Mercer: Oh, they have been awfully good about it. My eldest boy, he was eleven when Philip was born, and I made my husband tell the children before I came home. I knew very well I was going to be in tears and they would ask why, so I made him tell Richard first, and Richard sat and listened to him and then he said, "Can we keep him?" In fact, they have been marvellous about him and so have their friends.

Hannam: How do they treat him?

Mrs. Mercer: Indulgently. The boy who is twelve now, he got to the model-making stage at the age of six and Philip would sometimes get in the way, and then of course there would be a great hoo-ha about it; but they are very fond of him, very tolerant, and very forgiving; they all look after him, too. Everybody has got their eyes and ears open for doors and things like

the same room as him. He is nine now and it is very difficult to get him from place to place because he wants to see all the same things all the time, like raindrops; he sits on the pavement watching the drops. His favourite animals are horses, cows, and sheep.

David is a very mischievous boy. His usual trick is trying to get the biscuits out of the tin on the shelf; another one is getting into my bed. He also jumps on me and fights. He likes banging on his drum and makes us all go mad. He had a guitar for his birthday and he plays that. It is very difficult for Mummy and Daddy because they don't understand him.

When we go on holiday without him I feel very sad because I miss his snoring, which stops me from having bad dreams. There is only one other boy who can cope with him and that is Adam Steele. He is the son of a doctor. David is very fat because he eats lots of bread and butter and biscuits [cookies]. I have known David longer and I like him a bit better than Toby [younger brother, aged four and a half]. We have some people who help with taking David for walks and help us. They are very nice to David.

Charles Hannam, the father of David and Simon, comments: "As far as I can tell, Simon does not seem in any way deprived or held back because he has a mentally handicapped brother. He realizes that he has some responsibility for David. We sometimes fear that we ask him to do too much, but Simon likes his responsibility: 'It is very difficult for Mummy and Daddy because they don't understand him.' I know what he means; we are often intolerant and angry, and it may very well seem to him that we don't treat his brother very well. David in some ways is an ideal brother: he is not competitive, and everything Simon does is bound to be better." In this family David's handicap clearly is not a problem for

Simon. Is it always so trouble-free for a child growing up with a handicapped sibling? Children with handicapped siblings are likely to take on roles and responsibilities that those with normal siblings don't have. They are also likely to have parents under considerable stress. What are the consequences of this responsibility and stress for the normal children? What kind of relationships do normal and handicapped siblings have?

The first point is that older siblings, girls especially, take on responsibilities for caring for their handicapped siblings, and that these responsibilities frequently have high costs for the normal children. This general finding turns up in studies of a number of different handicaps. In the 1950s, Farber carried out a series of surveys of the siblings of mentally retarded children. These were based on the *mothers'* views of the effects on their normal children (and therefore were not as objective as some of the more recent studies). According to the mothers, both brothers and sisters of the handicapped children showed high levels of frustration, tension, and anxiety, but it was the *sisters* whose handicapped sibling was at home who assumed more of the caregiving than the brothers and who suffered most. The degree of tension was highest among those who played the greatest part in caring for the handicapped child. In contrast, among the boys, those whose handicapped sibling was in an institution showed more tension than those whose sibling remained at home.

The fact that sisters of handicapped children suffered more than brothers was stressed in another study—one which drew on the memories of college-aged students' childhood experiences. In families in which there had been open discussion of the handicap and in which the children had expressed much curiosity about the handicap, the children coped more effectively in their adult

years. Those who had spent a lot of time in interacting with the handicapped sibling expre liking for the sibling as adults. And those wh icapped sibling had early been sent to an instit more difficulty in coming to terms with the than those whose handicapped sibling had rer home with them during their childhood. The ers concluded that if the family resources were to cope with the demands of a handicapped ch out placing undue hardship on the older siblin the normal children often adapted better—expe less guilt and unhappiness—when the handicapp remained at home than when they were instit ized. Charles Hannam points out that it is frighter small children if one of their siblings is sent awa institution. If it can happen to her, they think, it can happen to me, too.

In some families the normal children resist an gestion that their handicapped sibling should go residential unit—even for a brief spell. The follow excerpted from a dialogue between Charles Ha and the mother of six children. Philip, her young handicapped.

Hannam: Have you sent Philip to the residential unit the centre?
Mrs. Mercer: No. Never. No. The main objection com from my children. There is a great cry of "If he we normal you wouldn't dream of doing that." I su gested it when we were going to my niece's twent first birthday party; they said they could cope and said, "No, I think I'll put Philip into the residentia unit." "Don't you dare," they said; "he doesn't leave until we go to school. We can wait for the bus. We are home before he comes home." . . . We wouldn't dare put him in for a holiday because they adore play-

> this. The girl who is next to him in age, she is partic-
> ularly fond of him. They rush into each other's arms
> when they have been apart for a day.

The costs for older sisters of caring for a sibling with Down's syndrome are often heavy. Especially vulnerable are the sisters of Down's syndrome children in families that are struggling with other difficulties—many children, marital difficulties, or social problems. Often in these families the girls spend a great deal of time either caring for the handicapped sibling or the other normal children in the family. The stress shows up in rebellious and difficult behavior, especially at school.

Parents of Down's syndrome children often expect much more of their normal children than parents of other children—requiring a greater contribution to the housework and a higher degree of "socialized" behavior. The siblings of Down's syndrome children tend to have more behavior problems than the siblings of normal children; however, Ann Gath's longitudinal study of families with Down's syndrome children showed that this was related to problems in the marriage of the parents. The family stress showed up first in the marital difficulties and in parental psychiatric disorder, and only later in the normal siblings' behavior problems. The problems, which were the result of "acting out" rather than of misery or depression, appeared only in the families in which the Down's syndrome child also had behavior problems.

Ann Gath also studied families with children who suffered from handicaps other than Down's syndrome. Here she found that there was a greater incidence of behavior problems among the siblings of the handicapped children than among the siblings of the Down's syndrome children. Why were these children particularly vulnerable? There were differences in the family situations and social backgrounds of the two groups. The mothers of the handicapped group were younger, were experiencing a higher rate of marital breakdown, and were from lower social-class backgrounds. The family stress in these families was probably much higher than in the families with Down's syndrome children.

In trying to understand what the experiences of growing up with a handicapped child means for a sibling, we have to take into account the way in which the whole family responds to the stress, rather than simply consider the effect of the child on the sibling. The poignancy of the family situation and the difficulty for the siblings in particular are all too clear in this conversation with a mother of five children, one of whom has a brain injury.

Mrs. Richards: You know, it has caused quite a lot of problems in our family. I have a little boy, he is eight now. My husband has no time for him at all because he is all Jill now. He very seldom talks to Bill unless it's to tell him off, and Jill, like most mentally retarded children, is very affectionate, very loving, although in the next minute she can be spiteful. My husband expects Bill to accept all this. Well, you can't expect a normal healthy boy of eight to take all this and have his hair pulled. So of course he will give her one back, then my husband will have a go at him, then I have a go at my husband, and that's how it goes on.

Hannam: How do the older ones see it?

Mrs. Richards: Well, naturally they spoil her as well, but they haven't pushed out Bill either.

Hannam: Do they make it up to him a bit?

Mrs. Richards: Well they try, you know. I try to . . . there are some times I feel I could give him one when he is

> naughty or playing up, but I don't. I think, well, if
> Dad is always on to him, Mum can't be. He has got
> to feel someone loves him and wants him. So it is
> creating problems all round. I don't think people re-
> alize the problems it creates.

Caring for a handicapped sibling clearly causes difficulties. Children may also be concerned about the stigma
of having a sibling who is "different," who may behave
strangely or in a "naughty" way. One of the families
that Hannam describes in his book consists of two children—Brenda, a seven-year-old, and her five-year-old
sister Mary, who has a brain injury. Brenda is made
very anxious by the "dreadful" things her sister does,
and keeps on saying, "Mummy, look what Mary is
doing." On the other hand, many children will stand
up for their handicapped siblings in a most moving way,
when other children make disparaging remarks. One
child effectively dealt with another child who had said
"Your sister's daft" by retorting, "Not as bloody daft as
you'd be if you had an extra chromosome."

We know little about the relationship between siblings
when one of them is blind or deaf. A study of the older
siblings of preschool-aged deaf children showed that
although these older siblings had greater childcare responsibilities and fewer social activities outside the family than most children, this situation was mainly due to
differences in the kinds of families which the deaf children came from, rather than to the disability of the deaf
children. We know nothing of how children cope with
the stress of chronically or terminally ill siblings or of
how they cope with the changes in family relationships
that accompany the birth of a premature sibling. Clearly
research is needed into these questions, which have
practical implications for so many families under stress.

SIBLINGS AS THERAPISTS AND SOURCES OF SUPPORT

The brothers and sisters of children with problems can in some cases help them in a specific way, by acting as "therapists." A few clinicians have worked with the families of children with behavior problems, training the siblings as well as the parents to use behavioral techniques. The siblings learn to encourage and reward ("reinforce") particular behaviors shown by the problem child, and to discourage others. These interventions were *more* successful when the siblings took part than when only the parents were involved. Not only did the behavior of the problem child improve, but the relationship between the siblings changed for the better. Cooperative play between the children increased considerably. Most strikingly, the behavior of the sibling "therapist" *also* improved, and this was not because the parents had changed their behavior toward the therapist child. Rather, it seems that the experiences of the child therapist in training his or her sibling led to the improvement.

Siblings can also play a very important supportive role to children under stress. We saw in Chapter 2 that children who have to spend time in institutions or residential care apparently suffer much less if they are accompanied by a sibling. In a classic study, Anna Freud and Sophie Dann observed six orphans who had been brought up together in a German concentration camp during World War II. The children showed enormous loyalty and support toward one another when they were released after the war and spent time in a therapeutic nursery in England. "The children's unusual emotional dependence on each other was borne out further by the almost complete absence of jealousy, rivalry and competition . . . Since the adults played no part in their emotional lives at the time, they did not compete with each other for favors or recognition . . . They did not grudge each other their possessions . . . When one of them received a present from a shopkeeper, they demanded the same for each of the other children, even in their absence . . . At mealtimes handing food to the neighbor was of greater importance than eating oneself."

Supportive loyalty between siblings is vividly illustrated in Stephen Bank and Michael Kahn's account of the relationship between a nine-year-old girl and her six-year-old brother, who were living together in a foster home, awaiting adoption. The two were nearly inseparable, to the point where their social worker feared that they would never learn to function independently.

> *Interviewer:* What have you observed of their relationship?
> *Social worker:* Len [the little boy] makes no independent decisions without consulting her; even over a matter about what they are going to have for lunch or buy at the store, or anything that he has a question on, he will turn to her to get reassurance, a nod, approval, or whatever. He would rather turn to her than to the foster mother.

These same children shared the worry that, if separated, the little boy might collapse or get into serious trouble. When, in the interview, the idea of separate adoptions [separate homes] was introduced, he became visibly anxious, ran around the room and hid his head under the pillow. The little girl who, since the age of three, had considered herself his caretaker, worried constantly about this hyperactive youngster, *especially* when they couldn't be near one another.

Older sister: Sometimes, when I'm away from him, and he is somewhere else, I think about him.
Interviewer: Oh, well, what do you think about him when you are away from each other?
Older sister: That . . . I wish he was with me so that I could see him more and talk to him more.

This girl lived with the daily apprehension that her brother would act "bad" if not supervised closely by her. In restaurants, when he would go to the bathroom, she would worry about his getting lost on the way back to the table. Upon hearing that he had, once again, gotten into trouble, she would monitor him even more closely and assume even greater responsibility for his activities and whereabouts.

Bank and Kahn point out that there were disadvantages and problems for the little girl who had taken on these responsibilities:

This nine-year-old girl was becoming an old lady before her time, and although able to relate sensitively as an "adult," she seemed unaware of the world of play. At nine, she had found herself burdened with the care of her little brother and she appeared well on her way to a life of serious overresponsible behavior and grim perfection. Even though there was reciprocity in the relationship, and he verbalized his love for his sister, her sleeping and waking life was so preoccupied with worry about him that she often withdrew from contact with other people. In order to forget her worries about her brother she would (to quote her) "read a good book so I can get my mind off of him!" Although she loved him and he could be loving to her, she frequently verbalized frustration and rage about his behavior. She seemed to feel that his obnoxiousness and immaturity were a life-long burden that she would willingly but resentfully carry for a lifetime. In her case, the loyalty appeared to be lopsided. Although they were attached to one another, it was up to *her* to make certain that the other conditions of loyalty (such as cooperation, sacrifice, quick conflict resolution) were maintained. In short, by giving, she was becoming *depleted*. She appeared relieved when she learned that she and her brother would be adopted by separate families.

The role of supportive sibling obviously has its costs, even in the much less extreme cases of children in large families that include a handicapped sibling. Here are the comments of two people who have studied and helped such families. Ann Gath summarizes the findings on the siblings of Down's syndrome children: "Most of the Down's syndrome children in the studies mentioned have had a warm and friendly relationship with their siblings. They were responsive to the family atmosphere, showing appreciation of treats and presents. There is increasing evidence from a number of studies that parents can be trained as effective therapists for their own retarded children, and it appears from preliminary finds that involvement in such training programs is rewarding for the family as a whole and can lessen the chance of discord or lasting emotional distress. Given adequate information and appropriate medical, social, and educational services, most families can adapt to having a child with Down's syndrome and are able to provide a loving home background capable of responding to the needs of that child and his normal brothers and sisters." And Charles Hannam concludes in his study of the brothers and sisters of handicapped children: "The mentally handicapped child presents a burden that should not be put entirely on any one member of the family, particularly his brothers or sisters. It is important that they are allowed to entertain friends separately, should they wish to do so. Brothers and sisters may be under pressure that is not necessarily apparent to the parents. GPs, teachers, and social workers should be alerted to the possibility of stress once they know that there is a mentally handicapped child in the family."

This chapter has dealt with some of the practical problems that coping with siblings can present to parents. But it is worth reflecting for a moment on the implications these same problems have for the book's third theme: the picture of children's emotional and cognitive development that we gain from studying siblings. First, the overwhelming emotional impact of the presence of a sibling is poignantly demonstrated in the disturbed behavior which the majority of children show at their sibling's birth. It is evident, too, in the aggressive behavior between siblings. The emotional power of this relationship and its significance in the pattern of *family* relationships must in part explain why children are so sophisticated in understanding their siblings. It is an urgent matter—and clearly highly adaptive—for children to be able to "read" their siblings' intentions and moods. We must, of course, be cautious about inferring a causal link between parents' *talking* about the sibling as a person and decreased disturbance in the firstborn. Yet we should take seriously one implication of this finding: children are not only responsive to the feeling states and needs of their siblings, but are capable of *reflecting* on their feelings and wants. The understanding shown by siblings of handicapped children, the effectiveness of siblings as therapists, and the support that siblings provide for children in distress all reinforce the argument that the intimacy and emotional power of this relationship can foster remarkable capabilities in such young children. These findings suggest, too, that children can be encouraged and helped to support and care for their siblings—that individual differences in affection and concern for the sibling are influenced by the extent to which adults foster such caring behavior. We turn next to the origin of individual differences and to sibling influence, this time approaching the issues from a very different perspective—that of genetics.

8 / Heredity and Environment

To parents, the question of whether differences in children's personalities, talents, intelligence, physical qualities, athletic abilities, and behavior problems reflect genetic differences or differences in the ways in which the children have been brought up is an absorbing one. From the moment a baby is born, relatives and friends as well as parents are on the lookout for signs that "She's got your eyes," or "He's going to be a football player like his father." Many parents see some of their own characteristics in one or another of their children—sometimes with pride, sometimes with apprehension. Is this simply self-projection? What do scientific studies of the genetics of siblings and of twins tell us about this issue? We have already looked at some of the differences between siblings and at the questions these differences pose for psychologists. Here we consider in more detail the part that heredity plays in the similarities and differences between siblings, and see what genetic studies can tell us about the relative importance of environmental and genetic influences.

GENETIC SIMILARITY OF SIBLINGS

All humans share a major portion of their genes with one another—in fact, more than half of human genes are identical to those in other primates. "Heredity" refers not to these universal genes but to genes that differ among individual people, and to the fact that such varying genes are shared by blood relatives. Siblings are first-degree relatives, which means that they share roughly half of these genes. In contrast, pairs of randomly selected individuals will show only chance genetic similarity for these varying genes.

Take as a simple example of genetic transmission the blood types AB and O. A person's blood type is determined by the particular form of a gene that happens to be on the top of the ninth chromosome. A, B, and O are alleles, alternate forms of this gene. For any gene, a person has two alleles, one on each of a pair of chromosomes. Everyone has twenty-three pairs of chromosomes, and, for each pair, an individual receives one from his mother and one from his father. The ninth chromosome from his mother might have had an A allele and the matching chromosome from his father might have had a B allele; if so, the individual's blood type would be AB, which would mean that he could accept blood in a transfusion from a donor with any blood type.

Siblings have a fifty-fifty chance of having the same blood type. Although two genetically unrelated individuals *could* have the same blood type (because of the thousands of genes that vary among humans), the genetic similarity for pairs of these genetically unrelated individuals will center around zero, whereas, for siblings, genetic similarity will center around 50 percent. Now the complex behaviors that interest psychologists and parents, such as mental abilities, temperament, and psychopathology, are *not* affected by single genes as is the ABO blood system. No one knows how many genes affect such complex characteristics, but the numbers are likely to be in the hundreds at least. If individual differences for such characters were entirely due to genetic factors—which they are not—siblings would be 50 percent similar, and pairs of genetically unrelated individuals would not be similar at all.

The fact that siblings are 50 percent genetically similar is critically important for understanding the development of siblings and their relationship. Behavioral genetic research using the comparison of identical and fraternal twins as well as recent adoption studies makes it clear that quite a high proportion of the individual differences in mental abilities, temperament, and psychopathology are due to genetic differences among individuals. To the extent that these characteristics are genetically mediated, siblings will be similar. In fact, the research indicates that nearly all the similarity in personality characteristics within pairs of siblings is due to the siblings' genetic similarity rather than the fact that they share the same family environment.

Adoption studies have shown that when genetically unrelated children are adopted into the same family, and brought up in the same family from early in life, they are considerably less similar than biological siblings who share heredity as well as family environment. Furthermore, biological siblings reared apart from birth are only slightly less similar in IQ than siblings reared together.

This is not to say that the environment is unimportant—the same data provide some of the best available evidence for the importance of the environment. However, studies do show that the *family* environment shared by siblings does not make them very similar. The environment makes siblings in the same family *different* from one another, not *similar* to one another.

The most dramatic examples of the importance of genetics come from studies of identical twins—clones, from a genetic point of view—who have been reared apart from early in life. Studies by Thomas Bouchard at the University of Minnesota contain examples of uncanny resemblances between adult twins separated since birth. Some of the most striking similarities involve behaviors seldom studied by psychologists, including laughing style, gesticulation, mannerisms, and gait.

Although these genetic "bonds" are less noticeable in siblings brought up together in the same family, we certainly should not ignore the part that genetic similarities may play in influencing the sibling relationship. For example, recent research has shown that biological siblings perceive themselves as having a closer, more loving, and more understanding relationship than adopted siblings. This could be in part because adopted siblings usually know that they are adopted, while biological siblings know that they share a greater proportion of their genetic makeup. But this is unlikely to be the whole story. Genetically related siblings not only perceive themselves as more similar, but perceive the way their parents treat them as more similar. They also see their own treatment of each other and the way their peers behave toward them as more similar than do adopted siblings. What this means is that the influences which we usually think of as *environmental*—the effects of parents, siblings, and peers—are affected by the *genetic* similarity of the siblings.

Siblings are likely to be genetically more similar to each other than they are to their parents. The reason for this is that parents share with their offspring only that portion of genetic variance that "breeds true" (called "additive genetic variance"), whereas siblings share both additive and nonadditive genetic variance. Using the ABO example again, a parent can give an offspring only one allele, A, B, or O. However, these alleles do not simply add up in their effect on the blood type—an O allele, for example, counts for nothing when combined with an A allele or a B allele. Siblings have a 50 percent chance of receiving the same allele from each parent, which means they have a 25 percent chance of getting the same *combination* of alleles from their parents. Thus, nonadditive effects such as those for the ABO blood system are shared by siblings but not by parents and their offspring.

GENETIC DIFFERENCES AMONG SIBLINGS

The first law of genetics is that like begets like; the second law is that like does not beget like. Too often we think of heredity only in terms of similarity—heredity means that a trait "runs in the family"—rather than recognizing that heredity also means that siblings will be different from one another. For parents, genetic differences are likely to be more noticeable than genetic similarities because similarities can be detected only in relation to the rest of the population, whereas sibling differences are obvious in the day-to-day contrast of siblings in a family. It has been said that most people look for "environmental" explanations of children's behaviors *until they have more than one child:* it is easy to explain a first child's propensities environmentally—"the child is shy because we went out so seldom"—but such explanations fall away when the second child proves to be very different from the first.

An interesting twist to an already complicated picture is that some siblings are genetically more similar than others. Parents share precisely half of their genes with their offspring—they either give their child one chromosome or the other of each of the 23 pairs of chromosomes. Siblings, on the other hand, are 50 percent similar genetically only on the average. For each chromosome pair, siblings have a fifty-fifty chance of receiving the same chromosome from each parent. Theoretically, then, it is possible for some sibling pairs to receive all of the same chromosomes, which would make them genetically identical; and some sibling pairs may receive none of the same chromosomes. It is likely that the common range of genetic similarity is only from 40 percent to 60 percent; nonetheless, this range represents a substantial effect. Thus, if it is true that genetically related siblings experience a closer relationship, then some sibling pairs will be closer than other pairs for genetic reasons.

TWINS

Most of what we know about genetic influence on development has come from studies of twins. Twins are not nearly as rare as is generally supposed. In most of the world, one in eighty-five births is a twin birth, although the rate of twinning, especially fraternal twinning, is affected by factors such as maternal age and fertility drugs. There are two types of twins. Fraternal twins are simply siblings who happen to be born at the same time—they develop from separately fertilized eggs. Identical twins are produced by a single fertilized egg that splits into two clones. About one third of the conceptions that produce twins result in opposite-sex fraternal twins, one third in same-sex fraternal twins, and the remaining third in identical twins. Twins provide a natural experiment for scientists in the sense that identical twins are genetically identical to each other and fraternal twins, like nontwin siblings, are 50 percent similar genetically on the average. Both types of twins are the same age, reared in the same family, born from the same womb, and are of the same sex in the studies used. In terms of physical characteristics such as eye color and height, identical twins are nearly identical and fraternal twins are about 50 percent similar, suggesting nearly complete genetic determination of these individual differences.

In fact, physical characteristics such as eye color and height can be used to determine whether twins are identical or fraternal. For parents, it is interesting to note that obstetricians who diagnose whether twins are identical or fraternal on the basis of the kind of placenta the twins have do so with little more than chance success. This is because about one third of identical twins (those that divide early before implantation, and implant in different places in the uterus) have separate chorions and amnions. In contrast, one can achieve greater than 90 percent accuracy in diagnosing the zygosity of the twins by asking a simple question that summarizes a host of *physical* characteristics: "Is it hard for strangers to tell the twins apart?"

In personality and behavior, identical twins are more similar than fraternal twins, although these traits are not nearly so greatly influenced by genetic factors as are physical traits like height. During the first year of life identical twins are, for instance, much more alike than fraternal twins in the degree to which they are shy or outgoing. Differences in activity in the first year, in contrast, do not seem to be genetically influenced. Yet in the second and third years, the similarity between identical twins *increases*.

Both parents of twins and twins themselves contrast

the twins in personality, exaggerating the differences between them. Identical twins reared apart are in fact more similar in personality than are twins reared together. This "contrast effect" shows up, too, in studies of parental descriptions of twins. These often yield *negative* correlations between the parents' ratings of their fraternal twins—implying, for instance, that one twin is labeled as the "active" one and the other as the "lethargic" one, even though compared to other children the twins are quite similar in activity level. Klaus Minde, a clinician studying the relationships between mothers and their twins, finds that it is very common for mothers to "prefer" one twin to the other from birth, meaning they respond very differently to the two, and that this apparently has no deleterious effect on the way in which both children's attachment to the mother develops.

CHANGES IN GENETIC INFLUENCE DURING CHILDHOOD

The dramatic differences between children within the same family may, as we've seen, in part result from differences in parental treatment, in part from children's exploiting different aspects of the family environment ("ecological niche-picking"), and in part from the direct influence of the siblings upon one another. Sandra Scarr has argued that in middle childhood and adolescence the importance of the "active niche-picking" process as a source of the differences between siblings increases. In infancy, she suggests, a baby can selectively attend to what the adults provide, but cannot actively affect or choose his environment to nearly the same extent as he can when he is an older child or adolescent.

Older children and adolescents have many more op-
portunities than infants and younger children to actively
seek out and select their own environments. Both at
home and in the larger world, older children can make
their preferences known. Most parents are responsive
to the different interests and talents of their children:
Siblings who like to read are more likely to receive books
as gifts; those who prefer sports are more likely to receive
sports equipment. Siblings who are good at mathematics
are more likely in high school to take advanced math
courses than others whose interests and talents lie in
languages. And so forth. Older children can be more
active in establishing genotype-environment correlations.

In discussing this argument, Scarr draws attention to
some very striking and provocative findings on the
changing similarity between siblings and twins as they
grow from infancy to adolescence. She points out that
studies of fraternal twins who are followed from infancy
to adolescence show that the similarity between the children in IQ *decreases* from infancy to adolescence. And
the similarity between adolescents who were adopted
in infancy is very low indeed: − .03, as compared with
the correlations of .25 to .38 of adopted siblings in early
and middle childhood.

How can it be, Scarr asks, that the longer siblings live
together, the less alike they become? She stresses that
in middle childhood and adolescence the power of individual children to choose their own environment within
the family increases. For adopted siblings, this means a
move "from an early environment, in which the mother
may have produced intellectual similarity, to environments of their own choosing. Because their genotypes
are hardly correlated at all, neither are their chosen en-

vironmental niches. Thus, by late adolescence, adopted siblings do not resemble each other behaviorally."

At present, we have only evidence for these changes with age in IQ. The extent to which similarities in personality between biological and adopted siblings change as the siblings grow into adolescence remains an intriguing and unanswered question.

Studies of the similarities and differences between siblings have important implications for our theories about why individuals develop in the ways that they do. The differences in personality between siblings brought up together suggest that the family and child-rearing variables usually assumed to be of major importance do not in fact explain much of the variance between individuals. Comparisons of biological and adopted siblings suggest that the influences that we usually think of as "environmental"—the effects of parents, siblings, and peers—are affected by the genetic similarity of the siblings, and that the relative importance of genetic and environmental influences may well change as children grow into adolescence.

9 / Continuities

We have looked so far at the way young sisters and brothers get along, at their quarrels and play, their dislike and affection for one another during the early years. The emotional power of the sibling relationship in these childhood years is clear. But to answer the general question of how far siblings influence each other's development, we must look beyond childhood. The majority of people have living siblings until the end of their lives. Are closeness and affection between siblings in childhood the beginnings of a warm relationship that continues to be affectionate and close throughout adulthood? Do the rivalries of the first years disappear?

We know that for some, at least, the rivalries of early childhood persist till death. Henry James wrote that his brother William "had gained such an advantage of me in his sixteen months' experience of the world before mine began that I never for all the time of childhood and youth in the least caught up with him or overtook him. [William was] always round the corner and out of sight, coming back into view but at his hours of extremest ease. We were never in the same schoolroom, in the same game, scarce even in step together or in the same phase at the same time; when our phases overlapped, that is, it was only for a moment—he was clean

153

out before I had got well in." Leon Edel, in his biography
of Henry James, points out that "the image of an absent,
elusive, distant William persisted to the end. The nov-
elist 'seems often to think that my father is here, *tho'
not in the same room,*' William's oldest son wrote during
Henry James's last illness." How common is this per-
sisting pattern of a relationship that begins in early childhood?

In the early school years the comfort and support,
rivalry and conflict, of the relationship between siblings
are not only still evident, but show clear links with the
earlier relationship between the children. In the Cambridge study of the effects of the sibling's birth, the
differences in firstborn children's interest in and affection for their newborn sibling showed a consistent relation to the striking individual differences in the quality
of the relationship which developed between the siblings over the years that followed. The two- and three-
year-old children who were friendly to their fourteen-
month-old sibling and who talked to their mother in an
affectionate way about their sibling were, as six-year-
olds, much more likely to describe their sibling in warm,
positive terms than the children who in the earlier years
had behaved in a hostile way toward their sibling.

This finding is a striking one. The six-year-olds had
entered the world of peers and school and had made
the transition to a whole new set of experiences, yet
their relationship with their siblings had remained, in
emotional terms, very stable. What happens as the children grow up? How do the changes of adolescence and
young adulthood affect the relationship between young
siblings? No one has followed siblings from childhood
to adulthood, so all we can draw upon are the memories
that people have of their childhood relationships and
their impressions of how these developed or changed.

However, although we lack good longitudinal information, we do know something of how people feel about their siblings at different stages of the life cycle, and we know to what they attribute the closeness or rivalry that they feel. Some of the retrospective studies give us a vivid picture of the significance of the relationship between siblings during adolescence. It is clear from the accounts that adults give, when they are exploring their feelings of warmth and closeness with their siblings, that middle childhood and adolescence were often a time in which the brothers and sisters grew particularly close. Teaching, supporting, and imitating each other, "exploring issues through intense discussion, even providing dates for each other were all relatively frequent. Through these interactions close personal relationships developed."

Letters written by adolescents to their siblings show us, too, the closeness and intimacy that can develop between brothers and sisters at this stage. Mozart used his older sister, Nannerl, as a *postillon d'amour* by whom he sent messages to his girlfriends, and he kept up a stream of joking, ridiculous, mocking, but very affectionate letters to her. Here are the endings of two of his letters written when he was sixteen: "Farewell my little lung. I kiss you, my liver, and remain as always your unworthy frater brother Wolfgang." "Please. Please, my dear sister, something is biting me. Do come and scratch me. To my sister I send a pockmark of a kiss." A year later, in 1773, he wrote:

I hope, my queen, that you are enjoying the highest degree of health and that now and then, or rather, sometimes, or better still, occasionally, or, even better still, qualche volta, as the Italians say, you will sacrifice for my benefit some of your important and intimate thoughts, which ever proceed from that very fine and clear reasoning power, which in addition to your beauty, and although from a woman, and particularly from one of such tender years, almost nothing of the kind is ever expected, you possess, O queen, so abundantly as to put men and even greybeards to shame. There now, you have a well-tuned sentence.

Farewell,
Wolfgang Mozart

The importance of the relationship between brothers and sisters during adolescence is referred to again and again in the reminiscences in James Bossard and Eleanor Boll's study of large families. The siblings helped each other through many of the experiences of adolescence and emerging sexuality, making and keeping friends, getting and holding jobs. In contrast, it seems that closeness between siblings rarely *begins* in adulthood, though it is usually *maintained* throughout adulthood. The closeness and affection between siblings in late adulthood and old age are particularly marked. Victor Cicirelli has carried out a series of studies of adult siblings, at all stages of life. He showed, among other things, that college-aged siblings felt emotionally more positive toward their siblings than toward their fathers, and in several respects felt closer to their siblings than to their mothers. In middle age, 68 percent of the individuals felt close or extremely close to their siblings, and only 5 percent not close at all. And in old age, 83 percent felt close or extremely close to their brothers and sisters.

What kind of "closeness" did these brothers and sisters feel for each other in adulthood and in old age? First, a great deal of *interest* in each other, and a feeling that this interest is mutual. However, the feelings of closeness and compatibility did not often seem to extend to confidences and intimacies of a deeply personal sort. Only 8 percent of the middle-aged siblings that Cicirelli interviewed said that they would discuss important decisions with their siblings frequently, and 36 percent said that they would rarely if ever discuss intimate topics with their siblings. Yet intense closeness between adult siblings is apparent from the letters of some of our most well-known writers. Stendhal's letters, for instance, reveal how tenderly he loved his sister and how close he felt to her as an adult: "Everything you say," he wrote to her, "is in complete harmony with what I feel. You are absolutely my *alter ego*." And in another letter he tells her, "I love you with all my soul. I shall never love a mistress as I love you."

Rivalry between brothers and sisters also continues in adulthood and old age, as we saw from the quotations from Henry James, though the studies disagree about how common it is. Brothers apparently report more competitiveness than sisters, and the rivalry is particularly acute if the brothers are at different occupational levels. The processes of comparison—use of the sibling as a yardstick by which to measure success—that were evident in childhood clearly continue. But rivalry seems to decrease as the brothers and sisters grow into middle and old age. Some people argue that this decrease reflects the lack of contact between adult siblings. They suggest that if siblings were forced to live together or work closely together, the feelings of rivalry would reappear. When rivalrous feelings toward the siblings are probed with in-depth interviews, the results suggest that many adults (45 percent in one study) do still feel rivalrous with their brothers and sisters. These feelings seem to reflect the childhood patterns of rivalry continuing into adulthood. They are, for instance, often reactivated when relationships with the parents are directly involved. Preferential treatment by parents, favoritism, and overt or covert comparison by the parents cause conflict between adult siblings just as they did with young children.

Sigmund Freud strongly believed that rivalry persists between adult siblings: "I do not know why we presuppose that that relation [of children to their brothers and sisters] must be a loving one; for instances of hostility between adult brothers and sisters force themselves upon everyone's experience and we can often establish the fact that the disunity originated in childhood or has always existed. But it is further true that a great many adults, who are on affectionate terms with their brothers and sisters and are ready to stand by them today, passed their childhood on almost unbroken terms of enmity with them." He stressed the frequency with which adults dream of the death of their siblings: "In none of my women patients, to take an example, have I failed to come upon this dream of the death of a brother or sister, which tallies with an increase in hostility."

CLOSENESS BETWEEN ADULT SIBLINGS

Where does the closeness between adult siblings originate? We could answer this question only if individuals were observed over time—and that has not been done. But there are two themes that stand out in the cross-sectional research on adults at different stages of life.

The first theme is the importance of the early experience of the brothers and sisters together. Again and again people who are close to their siblings as adults maintain that the shared experiences of childhood and adolescence, the experiences of being part of a close family, are central to the affection that they feel for their siblings later in life. Closeness seems to be particularly marked in those families in which the children played together, ate together, shared bedrooms, went to school together, attended church together. Sixty-eight percent of the people from large families in Bossard and Boll's study described their relationships with their brothers and sisters as adults in terms such as "very close," "strongly knit," "seeing each other as often as we can," "sticking together," and "helping each other." Those people who as children had played together all or most of the time were especially likely to be very close as adults, and those who had not played together as children had very little contact with each other as adults.

Whatever doubts we may have about the limited samples examined in these studies and the retrospective methods, the implications of these findings are very important. The message is that what happens between brothers and sisters in the early childhood years is of real significance to people in their seventies and eighties.

The second theme that recurs in the studies of adult siblings is that critical events in the siblings' lives bring about important changes in the relationship. The dynamics of the relationship between brothers and sisters—the closeness and rivalry they feel—are crucially affected by events such as sickness, divorce, or death of the parents, or marriage of a sibling. These events affect the siblings' relationship whether they occur in adolescence, adulthood, or old age. The *nature* of the effect of critical events on the sibling relationship differs greatly from family to family. In a study by Helgola Ross and Joel Milgram, sickness of the parents led to negative consequences for the sibling relationship in the case of 56 percent of the siblings, but to positive change in the case of 44 percent. Marriage of a sibling enhanced closeness for 31 percent of the individuals, but led to negative change for 69 percent. Death of a parent when the siblings were children or adolescents had complex effects on the sibling relationship, but the sharing of pain and confusion led to increased closeness for most siblings. When parents died at an "expected" stage of life, or when a sibling died, the shared grief of the remaining siblings usually brought them together. Divorce of parents, however, led to increased conflict between some siblings, increased closeness between others.

Similar incidents apparently have very different consequences for siblings in different families. The effects of a critical incident on the relationship between siblings is linked to the quality of their relationship *before* the event. If siblings are close and affectionate, a critical incident often increases the closeness; if the relationship is hostile and rivalrous, a similar incident often exacerbates the conflict. There is a parallel here to the way in which family relationships before and after a second child's birth are linked to the firstborn's response to the baby sibling. There is also a parallel to the dynamics of the early sibling relationship: it is the degree of affection in the sibling relationship, rather than the sex or birth order of the siblings, that accounts for different effects of critical events on that relationship.

The importance of critical life events in the relationship between siblings and the significance of sibling support in moments of crisis can be seen in the following dialogues from Bank and Kahn's study. Two middle-aged brothers from a group of four are talking about their support for one another:

> *Youngest brother:* There's four brothers, going through life. Instead of falling apart, as many would do at a crisis—like the death of our mother or the crumbling of our father as a "figurehead" of the family, we didn't. We complemented each other. If one is down, the

others are up. At *no* time would all four of us be down, because whoever might be down at a particular time, it will be recognized by the others, and they would help to get him up.

Second-oldest brother: Whether that be financially or spiritually.

Youngest brother: Right! Regardless of what it is. For example, I know as I sit right here, if I ever got in any trouble—the *first* ones I go to is my brothers. I don't call my father. I don't call my in-laws. I don't *call my wife*. I call my brothers.

And here is a college-aged brother recalling the crises his younger brother had to cope with as a child:

Older brother: He had to encounter a lot of things that I didn't when I was growing up. A couple of things happened to him when he was younger. [His voice begins to tremble and he suddenly weeps, remembering.] He was in the hospital. I was upset. And it was like . . . [his voice breaks, unable to speak for a moment]—*I* was going through it. I felt that it was the worst thing that could happen to me. It was like sympathy. I felt pain for him. When he has an operation or goes into any adverse situation—it, it makes me cry.

Intense loyalty, support, and closeness between siblings are likely to develop, Bank and Kahn argue, with the loss or inaccessibility of a parent. Other studies of old age show that with the death of the mother, there is often a change in the relationship between brothers and sisters. Older sisters frequently take on the role of the mother in caring for the brothers in the family. Sisters sometimes assume the role of a brother's dead wife, too.

The closeness between siblings that most people report in late middle age and old age is presumably increased by the support that siblings provide in response to such incidents. Even though the origins of the affection between brothers and sisters may well lie in their shared experiences as children, the dramas and crises of adult life clearly help to enhance the siblings' closeness.

Bank and Kahn believe that the personalities of the individual siblings and the quality of parental monitoring of the sibling relationship in adolescence are also of major significance in the development of the relationship in adulthood. As in the childhood years, it is differences in affection and hostility between siblings, and the close connection between parent-child and sibling relationships—rather than simply age gap, birth order, and sex—that are of greatest developmental importance.

There are however, some differences between the sexes in the development of the sibling relationship in late adulthood and old age. Men with sisters express greater emotional security and happiness, and women with several sisters are most concerned with helping others and with maintaining social relationships and are better able to deal with criticism from others. Sisters are, it seems, particularly important in providing emotional support in adulthood, and they play a major role in keeping family relationships together over time.

Although we cannot yet say with precision to what extent siblings influence the development of adult personality, we do know that the power of the relationship lasts far beyond childhood. It withstands separations of time and space, and provides important emotional security for most people in the later stages of life.

Why should there be such closeness between siblings

in later life? Why should the relationship persist under circumstances of physical and temporal separation which would lead most friendships to fade? The stress that so many individuals lay on their shared childhood experiences gives us a clue. It suggests that contact with siblings in late adulthood provides not necessarily deep intimacy but a sense of belonging, security, attachment to a family. The tie between siblings provides an important buffer against the insecurity of aging and the loss of parents. The evidence that the sibling relationship is of real importance to the majority of individuals in old age, and that many people attribute this closeness to their siblings in adulthood to their early years together in the family, gives a special significance to our focus on the relationship between brothers and sisters in childhood.

10 / Conclusion

This book began with two general questions. The first was whether growing up with a sibling influences a child's development. The second was the question of why there are such striking differences in the quality of sibling relationships. What kind of answers have we gained?

The indirect effects of living with a sibling are clear. Growing up with a sibling has profound effects on a child's relationship with his or her parents, as is shown by the responses of children to the birth of a sibling and by the patterns of mutual influence in family relationships. If we assume that the parent-child relationship is important, then we should take seriously the impact of siblings upon that relationship.

Do siblings also affect one another directly in these early years? The answer strongly suggested by the distinctive features of their relationship is that they do. The nature of the relationship between siblings—emotional, intense, uninhibited, full of imitative behavior, steeped in an understanding of how this other person behaves and what will affect him—means that it is potentially tremendously important as an influence on a growing child. Hostile actions between siblings shape each child's aggressive behavior; the older sibling is often a model for the younger; older siblings introduce very young children to a shared world of fantasy play—a world that the latter simply cannot enter alone when so young. The comments that the children themselves make about their siblings suggest that these exchanges are far from trivial for each child.

But before we can assess the effects of growing up with a sibling, we have to recognize one crucially important feature of the relationship. This is the dramatically wide range of differences in the quality of the relationship between siblings. In some families every interaction is warm, supportive, playful, affectionate. In other families all exchanges are hostile, and in others the relationship is far more ambivalent. This means that while in general terms we can identify the ways in which children affect their siblings, and the areas in which they are likely to influence each other (aggression, social understanding, sex role identification), whether they *do* in fact exert such influence will depend on the emotional quality of their relationship, and on how this relationship fits into the pattern of the other relationships in the family. To describe the patterns of influence, we must acknowledge that it is not just a matter of generalizing from the birth order, age gap, or sex of the siblings. Rather, we must take account of the affectionate quality of the relationship, the children's personalities, and their relationships with their parents. In a sense, then, the book's first two themes—sibling influence and individual differences in siblings—are closely linked. We cannot get very far in addressing questions raised by the first without acknowledging the importance of the second.

Why do some siblings get along well and others not at all? The traditional way of thinking about this question and of explaining differences between siblings within a family has been to stress the importance of the birth order, age gap, and gender of the children. Yet the studies described here show that these are *not* the most important variables in accounting for differences in the affection, cooperation, aggression, imitation, hostility, or empathy shown by siblings in the preschool period, in middle childhood, or in adolescence. Birth order *is* important (unsurprisingly) in the dominance and the power relations between siblings, and in the kind of caregiving children offer their siblings; age gap, too, is important in these "parent-like" behaviors. And a first child's interest in and affection for his or her younger siblings has a powerful fostering effect on the relationship between them. But recent research strongly suggests that psychologists should think again before assuming that what matters most in a child's relations with his siblings are the traditionally favored factors of birth order, age gap, and gender.

For parents, the issue is of real practical importance. There is, as we have seen, evidence that the quality of the relationship between siblings is linked to each child's relationship with the parents. Although it would be unrealistic to try to draw practical rules of thumb from the finding that in families with an intense relationship between mother and firstborn daughter, the siblings are likely to be hostile, certain styles of parental behavior toward siblings probably do encourage supportive, affectionate behavior. Talking to each child about the other, explaining feelings and actions, emphasizing in a consistent way the importance of not hurting the other— all these appear to be linked to the development of a more harmonious relationship. At a down-to-earth level, the research on the arrival of a baby sibling suggests some straightforward practical ways for minimizing the first child's upset. However, individual differences in how well siblings get along are linked to many factors other than the parent-child relationship, and among the most important of these are two that a parent can hardly hope to influence: the children's gender and temperament. In the early years, hostility is often more common between siblings of different gender. It is important for parents to know just how common this hostility is— and for them not to feel primarily responsible for the aggression between their children. The fact remains that most firstborn children are at least ambivalent about their siblings, and quarreling is frequent and uninhibited in most families. Siblings do not choose each other. We should not be surprised that some should find it profoundly difficult to live together, forced as they are into daily intimacy.

This intimacy and the intense emotional quality of the relationship are crucial in explaining the third theme of this book: the striking picture of children's developing understanding of their world that we gain from watching siblings. Until now, the themes of competition and rivalry have dominated the literature on brothers and sisters. Recall Freud's assertion that even loyalty among siblings grows from their rivalry for parental love. But it is clear from watching and listening to young sisters and brothers, and from the writings of poets and novelists, that the relationship between young siblings is far more complicated, more affectionate, and much more interesting than this image of Cain and Abel would suggest. Children act toward their siblings as friends, supporters, comforters, and sympathetic playmates, and not only as bullies and aggressors. The complexity and diversity of their behavior toward their siblings reflect a striking depth of understanding and emotion. It is because they *understand* their siblings so well, and because they *feel* so strongly about them, that their relationship is so significant and so revealing. It is important to recognize how closely this understanding of the sibling and the emotional depth of the relationship are bound up. Sisters and brothers understand each other well not only because from infancy they have shared a familiar world and have been daily exposed to each other's ways and wishes, but also because of the emotional urgency of their relationship. It matters greatly to a child that he should understand what his sibling is feeling and intending to do.

The picture of children's powers of social understanding that is highlighted in the behavior of siblings together is one that in some respects conflicts with accepted views. For instance, the development of teasing and of children's responses to disputes between their siblings and their mother show that as early as sixteen to eighteen months, children develop a practical understanding of what will annoy *this person* or how to collude with and support *this person*. In the context of the sibling relationship, children also demonstrate an ability to comfort and to emphathize, to recognize and feel concern that another person is in distress, far earlier than was thought likely in such young children. With their siblings, children can cooperate within a pretend world, can contribute to a shared fantasy, can take on a pretend identity far earlier than was previously supposed. If we listen to what two- and three-year-olds say about their siblings, we hear comments on the other child's capabilities, feelings, intentions, and wishes—beliefs about another person that are not simply projections of the child's own perspective onto another. And in the descriptions that children aged five to seven give of their siblings—especially in their comments about what traits they dislike—we hear remarkably sophisticated and articulate accounts of another person.

The messages of this research are, first, that psychologists should not underestimate children's capabilities by studying the children only in situations that are unfamiliar to them or that have little meaning for them. Second, and even more important, it must be recognized what a crucial role emotion may play in the development of understanding, and vice versa. There is a far more general lesson here than simply the message that children understand their siblings well: what is important is the issue of *why* they understand them so well. We return here to the link between the emotional depth of the sibling relationship and the children's understanding of the sibling. In trying to explain why children at such an early age are able to grasp the feelings and intentions of their siblings, we should not ignore the emotional urgency of their relationship—the depth of affection, jealousy, or hostility. Children use their intelligence on what matters to them. The interest and the powers of social understanding demonstrated by these very young children in relationships with their siblings and their parents emphasize the point that learning to understand family members and the way they interact is of special adaptive significance.

To think of the relationship between sisters and brothers solely in terms of rivalry is, then, to oversimplify a relationship of distinctive and fascinating complexity. Let us let Cathy, a six-year-old from Cambridge, have the last word. "I like him," she says of her older brother Tom. "He's nicer than anyone. He takes me to school . . . He lets me play 'kick the can' with his friends . . . He's fun to do things with. We both like the same things. I'd be lonely without him. And . . . and . . . I like everything about him."

Works Cited
Suggested Reading
Credits
Index

Works Cited

Abramovitch, R., D. Pepler, and C. Corter. "Patterns of Interaction among Preschool-Aged Children." In M. E. Lamb and B. Sutton-Smith, eds., *Sibling Relationships: Their Nature and Significance across the Lifespan.* Hillsdale, N.J.: Erlbaum, 1982.

Aksakoff, S. *Years of Childhood.* Trans. J. D. Duff. Oxford: Oxford University Press, 1923.

Bank, S., and M. D. Kahn. "Intense Sibling Loyalties." In M. E. Lamb and B. Sutton-Smith, eds., *Sibling Relationships: Their Nature and Significance across the Lifespan.* Hillsdale, N.J.: Erlbaum, 1982.

Bigner, J. A. "A Wernerian Developmental Analysis of Children's Descriptions of Siblings." *Child Development* 45 (1974): 317–323.

Bossard, J. H. S., and E. S. Boll. *The Large Family System.* Philadelphia: University of Pennsylvania Press, 1956.

Bühler, C. *The Child and His Family.* London: Routledge and Kegan Paul, 1940.

Calladine, C., and A. Calladine. *Raising Siblings.* New York: Delacorte, 1979.

Chodorow, N. *The Reproduction of Mothering.* Berkeley: University of California Press, 1978.

Cicirelli, V. G. "Siblings Helping Siblings." In V. L. Allen, ed., *Inter-Age Interaction in Children.* New York: Academic, 1976. For references to Cicirelli's numerous studies, see J. Dunn, "Sibling Relationships in Early Childhood." *Child Development* 54 (1983): 787–811.

de Beauvoir, S. *Memoirs of a Dutiful Daughter.* Trans. James Kirkup. New York: Colophon, 1955.

Dunn, J., and C. Kendrick. *Siblings: Love, Envy and Under-standing.* Cambridge, Mass.: Harvard University Press, 1982.

Dunn, J., and N. Dale. "I a Daddy: Two-Year-Olds' Collaboration in Their Pretend Play with Sibling and Mother." In I. Bretherton, ed., *Symbolic Play: The Development of Social Understanding.* New York: Academic, 1984.

Farber, B. For references to and discussion of Farber's numerous studies, see G. H. Brody and Z. Stoneman, "Children with Atypical Siblings: Socialization Outcomes and Clinical Participation." In B. Lahey and A. Kazdin, *Advances in Child Clinical Psychology,* vol. 6. New York: Plenum, 1982.

Freud, A., and S. Dann. "An Experiment in Group Upbringing." *Psychoanalytic Study of the Child* 6 (1951): 127–168.

Freud, S. *The Interpretation of Dreams.* London: Hogarth, 1953.

——*Group Psychology and the Analysis of the Ego.* London: Hogarth, 1955.

Furman, W. "The Qualitative Features of Sibling Relationships." Forthcoming, 1984.

Gath, A. "Down's Syndrome and the Family." In M. Burgio, F. Fraccaro, L. Trepolo, and U. Wolf, eds., *Trisomy 21.* Berlin: Springer-Verlag, 1981.

Ginott, H. G. *Between Parent and Child.* New York, Avon, 1969.

Haight, G. S. *George Eliot.* Oxford: Oxford University Press, 1978.

Hannam, C. *Parents and Mentally Handicapped Children.* Harmondsworth: Penguin, 1975.

James, H. Quoted in L. Edel, *Henry James: The Untried Years.* London: Hart Davis, 1953.

Koch, H. L. "The Relation of Certain Formal Attributes of Siblings to Attitudes Held toward Each Other and toward Their Parents." *Monographs of the Society for Research in Child Development* 25, no. 4 (1960): 1–124.

Lamb, M. E. "The Development of Sibling Relationships in Infancy: A Short-Term Longitudinal Study." *Child Development* 49 (1978): 1189–96.

Mead, M. *Growing up in Samoa*. New York: Dell, 1968.

Mozart, W. A. *Mozart's Letters*. E. Blom, ed. Harmondsworth: Penguin, 1956.

Newson, J., and E. Newson. *Four Years Old in an Urban Community*. Harmondsworth: Penguin, 1970.

———*Seven Years Old in the Home Environment*. Harmondsworth: Penguin, 1976.

Patterson, G. R. "The Aggressive Child: Victim and Architect of a Coercive System." In L. A. Hamerlynck, E. J. Marsh, and L. C. Handy, eds., *Behavior Modification and Families*. New York: Brunner/Mazel, 1975.

Ross, H. G., and J. K. Milgram. "Important Variables in Adult Sibling Relationships." In M. E. Lamb and B. Sutton-Smith, eds., *Sibling Relationships: Their Nature and Significance across the Lifespan*. Hillsdale, N.J.: Erlbaum, 1982.

Scarr, S., and S. Grajek. "Similarities and Differences among Siblings." In M. E. Lamb and B. Sutton-Smith, eds., *Sibling Relationships: Their Nature and Significance across the Lifespan*. Hillsdale, N.J.: Erlbaum, 1982.

Spock, B. *Baby and Child Care*. New York: Pocket Books, 1969.

Stendhal. *To the Happy Few: Selected Letters of Stendhal*. Trans. Norman Cameron. London: John Lehmann, 1952.

Stewart, R. B. "Sibling Attachment Relationships: Child-Infant Interactions in the Strange Situation." *Developmental Psychology* 19 (1983): 192–199.

———"Sibling Interaction: The Role of the Older Child as Teacher for the Younger." *Merrill-Palmer Quarterly* 29, no. 1 (1983): 47–68.

Stillwell, R. "Social Relationships in Primary School Children as Seen by Children, Mothers and Teachers." Diss., University of Cambridge, 1984.

Sutton-Smith, B., and B. G. Rosenberg. *The Sibling*. New York: Holt Rinehart and Winston, 1970.

Tolstoy, L. *Anna Karenina*. Trans. Constance Garnett. New York: Modern Library, 1950.

———*Childhood, Boyhood and Youth*. Trans. R. Edmonds. Harmondsworth: Penguin, 1965.

Whiting, B. B., and E. Pope-Edwards, eds., "The Effects of Sex and Modernity on the Behavior of Mothers and Children." Report to the Ford Foundation, 1977.

Zahn-Waxler, C., M. Radke-Yarrow, and R. A. King. "Child-Rearing and Children's Prosocial Initiations toward Victims of Distress." *Child Development* 50 (1979): 319–330.

Suggested Reading

SIBLINGS THROUGHOUT THE LIFESPAN

Lamb, M. E., and B. Sutton-Smith, eds., *Sibling Relationships: Their Nature and Significance across the Lifespan.* Hillsdale, N.J.: Erlbaum, 1982. This book contains a number of very interesting chapters on siblings at different stages of life. See especially the chapter by Bryant on middle childhood, those by Cicirelli and by Ross and Milgram on adulthood, the chapter by Bank and Kahn on intense sibling loyalties, and the chapter by Scarr and Grajek on the genetics of sibling similarities and differences.

CROSS-CULTURAL STUDIES

Barry, H., and L. M. Paxson. "Infancy and Early Childhood: Cross-Cultural Codes 2." *Ethnology* 10 (1979): 466–508.

Weisner, T. S., and R. Gallimore. "My Brother's Keeper: Child and Sibling Caretaking." *Current Anthropology* 18 (1977): 169–190.

PRESCHOOL-AGED SIBLINGS

Dunn, J. "Sibling Relationships in Early Childhood." *Child Development* 54 (1983): 787–811. A review of developmental psychological research on preschool-aged siblings.

GENETICS

Plomin, R., J. C. DeFries, and G. E. McClearn. *Behavioral Genetics.* San Francisco: W. H. Freeman, 1973.

CLINICAL PERSPECTIVE

Bank, S. P., and M. D. Kahn. *The Sibling Bond.* New York: Basic Books, 1982. Two clinicians discuss the emotional relationship between siblings, especially its influence on identity development.

Credits

TEXT

Excerpts from M. Lamb and B. Sutton-Smith, eds., *Sibling Relationships: The Nature and Significance across the Lifespan* (Hillsdale, N.J.: Erlbaum, 1982), are reprinted by permission of Lawrence Erlbaum Associates, Inc. Excerpts from Charles Hannam, *Parents and Mentally Handicapped Children* (Harmondsworth: Penguin Handbooks, 1980), pp. 60, 61, 64, 65, 71, copyright © Charles Hannam, 1975, 1980, are reprinted by permission of Penguin Books, Ltd.

PHOTOS

p. x: Donald C. Dietz (Stock, Boston)
p. 8:   Gabor Demjen (Stock, Boston)
p. 27:   Cary Wolinsky (Stock, Boston)
p. 42:   John Lei (Stock, Boston)
p. 68:   Owen Franken (Stock, Boston)
p. 90:   Elizabeth Crews (Stock, Boston)
p. 108:   Owen Franken (Stock, Boston)
p. 140:   Frank Siteman (Stock, Boston)
p. 152:   James R. Holland (Stock, Boston)
p. 164:   Mike Mazzaschi (Stock, Boston)

Index